FOOTSTEPS

IN

TIME

FOOTSTEPS IN TIME

A. Michael Warrington

Trafford Publishing
Bloomington, Indiana, USA

Order this book online at www.trafford.com
or email orders@trafford.com

Most Trafford titles are also available at major online book retailers.

Editor: Joan Templeton, JET Editorial Services
Secretary: Suzanne Redmond
Illustrations: C.M.T.
Front Cover: Keith Dinwoodie, KFD Consulting Services

Printed in the United States of America.

ISBN: 978-1-4251-1351-3 (sc)

Trafford rev. 10/22/2013

 www.trafford.com

North America & international
toll-free: 1 888 232 4444 (USA & Canada)
fax: 812 355 4082

To Helen

On life's bramble bush
I found a rose
My lovely English Rose

Lives of great men all remind us
We can make our lives sublime,
And, departing, leave behind us
Footprints on the sands of time.

Henry Wadsworth Longfellow (1807-1882)

I would like to thank my editor, Joan Templeton, for her expert guidance through the entire publishing process.

Grateful thanks to Suzanne Redmond; her superb secretarial skills and her assistance all the way from inception to completion of the book have been invaluable.

I'd also like to give tribute to C.M.T. for her insightful illustrations, which capture the essence of each subject so successfully.

Thank you to Michael Warrington Jnr. for proof reading and to Keith Dinwoodie for his invaluable assistance with the front cover, with scanning the pictures and his overall technical and computer expertise.

My mother and father

TABLE OF CONTENTS

Illustrations by C.M.T.

ANIMALS

My Dog

He is your friend, your partner,
    your defender, your dog.
You are his life, his love and his leader.
He will be yours, faithful and true
    to the last beat of his heart.
You owe it to him to be worthy
    of such devotion.

Source Unknown

Inscription on the Monument of a Newfoundland Dog

The first to welcome; foremost to defend.

Lord Byron (1788–1824), poet

God's humble instrument; though meaner clay, should share the glories
of that glorious day.

Source Unknown

—Proclaimed on the gravestone of Copenhagen, the horse that carried
    Wellington at the Battle of Waterloo.

I had often wondered if, like myself, animals felt little of the aging
process, so gradually sinister, so insidious yet ruthless in its work.
    Marking yet another year's passage, did they too feel no
different, no older? Did they bear the knowledge, experience and
wisdom of their years as I bore mine—a strange overlay on the child
within me. The child who never truly disappeared? Were their images

Man's Best Friend

Much loved dogs from my youth

Tinker

Mickey

**Mickey and his crooked tail from when I accidentally ran
over it with my scooter**

of themselves blended as mine were for me. A blur of young and old, past and present and running through it all, a constancy that I think must be the eternity of spirit?

Watching Bear, my dog, send his mind soaring after that tennis ball, I knew that for him, as well as for me, some part of him was forever young, capable of anything. As he struggled to right himself in the grass, I saw the surprise in his eyes, as if he too had been unable— or unwilling—to see himself as an old dog who would fly through the sky no more. I never again threw his ball high against the clouds: he never again leaped to meet it. Looking through my tears, I sadly brought into focus the reality of Bear, my old dog.

Bones Would Rain from the Sky, **Suzanne Clothier**, 2002

The noblest of all dogs is the hot dog: It feeds the hand that bites it.

Laurence J. Peter

Heaven's the place where all the dogs you ever loved come to greet you.

Source Unknown

ANN LANDERS

Dear Ann:

You asked teenaged girls to write and tell you the "lines" that were used on them by boys who were after sex. What a great idea!

I'm no teenager (I'm 22) but I thought you might be interested in the "lines" pitched at me over the past several years. Some of them were hilarious, others downright pathetic.

The serious "for real" lines started in the ninth grade. My favourite boyfriend was best pals with a guy who dated the most popular girl in school. He told me she "did it." That, of course, meant "it" was the thing to do. When he discovered that strategy didn't work he promptly switched to "If you loved me you would prove it." I told him if he loved ME he wouldn't make such demands.

Finally, he became adamant and said I HAD to give in because my stubbornness was lousing up his maturing process and giving him pimples. When I told him to buzz off he threatened to kill himself. The threat turned out to be as ridiculous as the rest of his garbage.

Then I started to date a fellow who was extremely considerate of my feelings but also very affectionate. When I made my position clear, he didn't pester me about sex. We necked a little, but he never tried to step beyond the boundaries I set up. After a few blissful months, Mr. Well-Behaved informed me I was going to have to share him with "Winnie" (a hot number) who wrote notes which made it plain she was ready, willing and able to "fulfil" him.

Off I went to college—still intact but getting curiouser and curiouser. The second day on campus I met Claude. He told me on our second date that dozens of girls had followed him from the swimming pool to his apartment lusting after his bod. Others were so aggressive (and hungry) they knocked on his door with bottles they couldn't open, dresses that needed to be zipped, furniture they couldn't move— anything to get past his front door and hopefully into his bed.

Then there was Horace, two years my junior, who wanted me to "teach him." And Bernie, who was dying to know if a political science major had anything that worked besides her brain. And Orval, a religious nut who had been instructed by God to "show me the way."

Funny thing, nothing wore down my resistance. The lines just made me run in the other direction. No girl wants to feel used, fooled or easy.

When I finally said yes, it was because a sensitive and caring young man made me feel valuable as a human being. He applied no gimmicks, no hogwash, no sales talk. I made up my own mind. It was beautiful. I'm glad I waited.

HAPPY PAST AND PROUD

Dear HAPPY:
The more things change—the more they are the same.

Ann Landers

CANADIAN RED CROSS MEMORIAL HOSPITAL

A Brief History

In 1914, during the Great War, the Astor family invited the Canadian Red Cross to build a military hospital for wounded soldiers on part of the family estate at Cliveden, Buckinghamshire, in England. (though the postal address was Taplow, Bucks, after the nearby village of that name.) The first hospital was built on this site with equipment from Canada.

In 1940, during the Second World War, the Canadian Red Cross built a new, larger hospital with more equipment. The hospital was named the Canadian Red Cross Memorial Hospital.

After the war, the hospital was donated to the U.K. for use as both a general hospital and a centre for research into rheumatism in children. In the following years the hospital gained a large maternity unit, and medical, surgical, paediatric and T.B. wards. The hospital was also a training school for nursing and midwifery.

Perhaps most notably, the hospital formed the Special Unit for Juvenile Rheumatism, which became world famous. The special unit was run by Dr. Eric Bywaters—a world-renowned teacher and acknowledged expert on the pathology of rheumatic and bone diseases.

The children who were admitted to the special unit came from all over England, suffering from Juvenile Rheumatism and Juvenile Arthritis (Still's Disease). Some of the children had to remain in the hospital for many months, sometimes as long as a year, and the unit employed teachers who were able to further the children's education.

Early trials comparing the efficacy of cortisone and aspirin were carried out in the hospital. It was found that over the long term aspirin was as effective as cortisone, though with less side effects.

The Canadians never lost touch with the hospital. Each time the Canadian Mounted Police took part in the Windsor Horse Show, they took time out to come with their horses and visit the hospital. Some of the children were able to sit on a horse with a Mountie holding onto them. The sight of the Mounties with their red uniform jackets made it a colourful and memorable occasion for the children.

The Mounties visit the Canadian Red Cross Memorial Hospital

Despite its enormous achievements in research into childhood rheumatism and arthritis, in the early 1980s the hospital suffered from Health Authority budget cuts and was closed in 1985. Subsequently the hospital buildings were abandoned, despite containing medical equipment and even patient records. The hospital became derelict and gathered quite a reputation locally for its state of disrepair and reputed hauntings. It was finally, sadly, demolished in 2006.

Those who worked there remember it with great affection.

Dr. A. Michael Warrington, the author, who worked there as a doctor, 1954–1955 and 1957

A Hospital Romance—Personal Story

In 1954, I arrived at the Canadian Red Cross Memorial Hospital to work as a house physician on the medical wards. It was a wonderful place to work. My chief was Dr. George Hadley, a consulting physician from the Middlesex Hospital in London. He came down from London two days a week to do rounds. The hospital's Special Unit attracted some famous visitors, and the working atmosphere was pleasant and most agreeable. There was a communal dining room where the doctors, consultants, matrons and nurses all dined together. Because this had once been a military hospital, the doctor's lounge was always referred to as the mess.

On occasion, the general medical wards were full to capacity. If we had someone who had to be admitted urgently we would phone the Special Unit to see if they had a spare bed. Sometimes they had a separate room at the end of the ward near the ward sister's office.

On one occasion, we had an older man with pneumonia for whom we had no bed. I phoned the Special Unit to see if they had a spare room. They had, so we went down to their ward and admitted our patient. When I sat at the desk to write up the appropriate orders, a young nurse came and stood beside me. I was immediately taken with her. It was a moment I will never forget. Although I had known lots of girls, having been in the army for over five years before studying medicine, I had never before seen anyone who made such an impression on me—nor have I since. She had blue eyes and an attractive trim figure in a nice uniform, which had an unusual silver belt buckle with a portcullis—the Heraldic Shield of the Westminster

Nurse Helen Bond R.N., 1952

Dr. A. Michael Warrington in the
grounds of The Canadian Red
Cross Memorial Hospital, 1954

Hospital in London where she had trained. But above all something shone through, and I knew this was someone I wanted to get to know. Being able to go out with her over the next few weeks would bring me to know if this was someone I wanted to be with forever.

After that fateful day, I used to see her occasionally in the Grand Corridor (as it was known) which ran the length of the hospital. I would say, "Hello" and she would reply very properly, "Good morning." How could I get to know her?

Fortunately, the doctors were planning to have a party in the mess with some music and dancing and a few drinks. I asked her if she would like to come and, most fortunately, she agreed. At that time I barely even knew her name, but she told me afterwards how she learned mine: After I had written up the orders and left the ward that first day, she'd tried to read my signature on the order sheet but couldn't. Since she had to write my name in the report, she phoned the switchboard and asked, "Who is Dr. Hadley's new house physician?"

Having barely got to know her, I thought I should invite her out to a movie before going to the party. For some funny reason I thought it would be more comfortable for her if I brought a friend, another doctor from the hospital. So the two of us went with her to a local movie in Maidenhead. Helen has often wondered afterwards why I brought a friend. Well, I really don't know—I just had the idea she would be more comfortable going out with me for the first time if we were not alone.

The day of the party arrived, and my formerly reliable old Riley car (1934 vintage) would not start. I asked the house physician on the Special Unit, with whom I had become friendly, if he could drive me down to Maidenhead to call for Helen. So, we both arrived on her doorstep. Her mother answered the door and thought that my friend was the chap who was going to take Helen to the party. Afterwards, Helen was to say, "I really don't know why my mother thought that. I wouldn't have gone out with him—he was shorter than me."

When Dick (for that was his name) heard that I had invited Helen to the party, he was a bit put out to say the least, "But she is on my ward—I was going to ask her."

So this was how I met the light of my life.

A. Michael Warrington

CANDLES AND FLOWERS

When I was a youngster, our family lived next door to St. Swithun's Catholic Church. I used to serve Mass every morning at 7:00 a.m. and on Sundays sang in the choir. High Mass was at 11:00 a.m. with the full choir and the organ and was always very well attended.

On the carpeted steps leading up to the main altar were several tiers of beautiful flowers in glass vases filled with water. Below the top row of flowers, there were three large candles on either side of the Tabernacle. My job was to navigate the steps leading up to the altar with a lighted taper in my hand. It was then a matter of leaning forward to light the candles sitting among the banks of flowers.

On one occasion, as I leant forward to light a candle, my arm came in contact with the top row of flowers. To my horror, the whole bank of flowers started moving slowly away from me! I went running down the steps to the front of the altar…too late. The top tier crashed onto the middle tier, which crashed onto the lower tier, and the whole lot—flowers, vases and water—came crashing down onto the steps! The congregation stared, spellbound, at this sudden unexpected diversion.

I went across to the door at the side of the altar where some steps led down to the sacristy. Father MacSweeney, the parish priest, was standing at the bottom of these steps. He was red in the face and, as I came down the steps, he yelled, "Get out! GET OUT!"

So I went into the change area, took off my cassock and cotta and left the church.

In due course I was forgiven and allowed to serve on the altar again.

A. Michael Warrington

_____

CHEAP THRILLS

At first I thought it was a passing fancy, a fling. I thought that I could do it a few times and forget about it.

My so-called friends kept telling me what a great experience and how harmless it was. I should have realized that they were already hooked and just looking for someone to do it with.

Wiser friends tried to warn me. They said it would become a habit, that I would become obsessed and have to do it more and more as time went on.

Unfortunately, I didn't listen. Now I can't stop thinking about it, when I can do it, where I will get the money to pay for it, whether my husband will find out that I have done it again.

The worst part is my children have started doing it too and, I have to confess, I encourage them. My husband doesn't like it, but he is powerless to stop us.

I still remember my first time. I was nervous and didn't know what to expect. But I soon caught on and did it twice more that same day. First it was with friends, now I often do it alone. Again and again I have tried to stop myself but I just can't.

I am drawn to the experience, completely helpless in my compulsion. First, I feel the faint stirrings of excitement. My pulse quickens; my breathing becomes rapid and shallow. My hands begin to tremble slightly in a fever of anticipation.

No, I am not out to experience a mind-altering drug fix or forbidden sexual thrills. My addiction is much more insidious.

They say the first step to recovery is admitting that you have a problem, so, I admit it.

I am a garage-sale addict.

Sometimes, as I prepare to rush out the door, route map firmly in hand, my husband will enquire mildly, "But darling, just what is it that you are looking to buy?"

"Well, how should I know," I reply testily. "It all depends what's there now, doesn't it?"

He just doesn't understand—it is not what one buys, it is the thrill of the chase.

He used to regard my garage-sale shopping as a harmless pastime. One of my less-endearing habits to be sure, but certainly not grounds for divorce.

Then one fateful day I left for a garage sale with my mother-in-law in tow and for once returned empty handed, but alone. I explained to my husband that I had had leave his mother holding onto a still-life painting that I wanted to buy. The woman having the sale wouldn't keep it for me otherwise, muttering darkly about people who promise but never return. I asked him for some money so I could buy the painting and retrieve his mother.

My husband, normally the most mild-mannered man in the world, sputtered incredulously, "You left my mother hostage at a garage sale?" I reassured him that she looked quite comfortable when I left, perched on an old steamer trunk with a battered umbrella for shade. I am sure that is not the reason she returned to England so soon afterwards. I mean, she liked the painting too.

After that my husband laid down the law. I was only allowed to spend the spare change in the house and family members were not to be left "in hock" under any circumstances. The painting, lovely over the mantle, is much admired by visitors who sometimes enquire where it was purchased. My husband's response is a dagger-like glare in my direction while I am forced to murmur sweetly, "Oh, one of those art print shops, I think, wasn't it dear?"

The rules for successful garage-sale shopping are like those for jet fighters. Come in low and fast, make a quick strike and get out. Hesitate and all is lost.

Once I let a beautiful suede jacket slip through my fingers. I had it in my hand but put it down when I became momentarily distracted by a slightly tarnished, but complete, set of silver teaspoons. By the time I looked back, another woman was wearing and happily paying for the jacket. I was tempted to rip it from her body, but realized in time that she was my daughter's preschool teacher. I still groan with envy every time I see her wearing it.

Another time I spied and rushed over to an antique oak dining table and chairs. I laid a hand on one of the chairs at the same time as one of my neighbours, another ardent garage-sale shopper. Neither of us was about to relinquish the prize. So, to prevent fisticuffs, the fellow holding the sale tossed a coin. To my delight I won the toss and the handsome set now graces my dining room. My neighbour, poor sport that she is, still doesn't speak to me, even though I only gloat about it in private.

Once I started shopping at garage sales, I began to realize how fascinating it is, rummaging around in other people's cast offs. Did that trim woman once wear these outsized bloomers? Does this ten years worth of Playboy magazines indicate his dwindling interest or her dwindling patience with his interest?

The dog-eared books are often especially eloquent in telling the family's story. The titles start with *College Algebra,* move on to *Dating in the 80s, The Joy of Sex, The Wedding Planner* and *Buying Your First Home.* Then, *Baby's First Year, Children: The Challenge* and sadly, too often, Making Your Marriage Work, followed by the *Self-Counselling Divorce Guide*, accompanied by a For Sale sign on the lawn.

Occasionally I pause between sales to ask myself why I continue to frequent garage sales. I believe the answer is that shopping has become a tedious, boring chore, bereft of any enjoyment or skill.

Where is the excitement in purchasing packaged items in a homogenous stack, each with price sticker so that you will know exactly how much to pay? I cannot imagine the salesclerks at Sears taking kindly to my desire to haggle furiously over the prices of their merchandise.

By contrast curiosity, perseverance and elite bargaining skills help to elevate the garage-sale experience to an art form. Heading out, not knowing what, or if, you are going to buy—now that's shopping.

I love rooting through the worn-out shoes, velvet paintings, rusty garden tools and chipped crockery. Suddenly, I find it. The vase of my dreams, almost new, at a fraction of the store price, and no GST to pay. Almost beside myself with excitement, I sidle casually up to the householder. "Uh, how much do you want for this old thing?"

She fixes me with a steely-eye. "Four dollars," she states firmly.

"Four dollars!" I exclaim in pseudo dismay, thinking, "What a bargain!"

"It was my grandmother's. It is an antique," she says defensively.

"How about two dollars?" I ask.

"Absolutely not," is the firm reply.

"Oh well," I sigh and move away, still holding the vase. Covertly we watch each other, circling warily like gladiators in a ring. Finally I see my chance as the garage sale winds down—I move in for the kill. Sighing heavily, I say, "Well, I might be able to offer you three dollars for this vase, if you throw in that bag of old tennis balls."

"Done," she says, smiling broadly.

Filled with exhilaration, I bear the vase home.

I try to sneak it in the back way, but unfortunately he is on to me now and lies in wait just inside the back door. His voice stops me in my tracks.

"What, pray tell, might that be?"

"It is an antique vase and I got it for only three dollars," I exclaim proudly.

"How wonderful," my husband replies dryly. "And does it have a purpose in life?"

Loftily, I state, "Well, I suppose one could put flowers in it, but antiques don't actually have to have purpose, they just, well, are."

Our home is now filled to the rafters with objects, antique and otherwise, that just are. Tables that need refinishing, lamps with tattered shades, musty old books, ornaments and knick-knacks spill out of every bulging cupboard.

My children, now willing accomplices, come with me on my forays, clutching their nickels and dimes. They triumphantly return home with a motley assortment of teddies losing their stuffing, broken toys and pieces of incomplete jigsaw puzzles.

We troop in with our treasures, tired but happy.

Feeding an obsession only makes it grow, so each weekend I am forced to range farther afield, needing to find bigger and better sales. As with any addiction, as long as it's a source of enjoyment, quitting is out of the question.

"Perhaps one day we should have a garage sale of our own," my husband said just the other day, gazing in dismay on the chaotic jetsam adorning every inch of our living space. "You know, clear the decks a bit."

"Oh, don't be ridiculous," I admonished. "Who on earth would be silly enough to pay good money for any of this old junk?"

The look he gave me was quite indescribable.

Pat Woods, Vancouver Nursing instructor and garage sale aficionada

----

CHILDREN

Children Get Intelligence from their Mothers

People may be getting things backward when they wish a baby its mother's good looks and its father's brains, an Australian geneticist said recently. Women carry the gene for intelligence on their X-chromosome and are solely responsible for passing it on to their sons, Gillian Turner said in an essay for the medical journal, *The Lancet*. She said men should temper hormones with logic when choosing the mothers of their children and go for brains rather than good looks.

Women were more free to choose their mates for their looks, Dr. Turner said, as they could be assured that brains come from the female side.

Reuters

If I Had My Child to Raise Over Again

If I had my child to raise over again
I'd build self esteem first and the house later.
I'd finger-paint more and point the finger less.
I would do less correcting and more connecting.
I'd take my eyes off my watch and watch with my eyes.
I would care to know less and know to care more.
I'd take more hikes and fly more kites.
I'd stop playing serious and seriously play.
I would run through more fields and gaze at more stars.
I'd do more hugging and less tugging.
I'd see the oak tree in the acorn more often.
I would be firm less often and affirm much more.
I'd model less about the love of power and more about the power of
    love.

Diane Loomans

Parents' Creed

And a woman who held a babe against her bosom said: "Speak to us of Children."

And He said: "Your Children are not your Children. They are the sons and daughters of life's longing for itself. They come through you but not from you, and though they are with you, they belong not to you. You may give them your love but not your thoughts, for they have their own thoughts. You may house their bodies but not their souls, for their souls dwell in the house of tomorrow, which you cannot visit, not even in your dreams. You may strive to be like them, but seek not to make them like you. For life goes not backward nor tarries with yesterday. You are the bows from which your Children as living arrows are sent forth."

Kahlil Gibran

Motherhood

The wife of a professional man among my acquaintances has given birth to ten children, all beautifully alive, and is now expecting her eleventh. Since the fashionable thing has been to have one, and adopt another for a companion for it, or to have at most three, I was interested to have a chat with her when I encountered her in the supermarket shoving a vastly heaped shopping wagon—provisions for her boundless family.

"They tell me a new one is on the horizon," I said.

"Yes," said the sturdy, bright-eyed woman in her late 30s. "And why not? I realize that many of my friends are aghast at the size of my family. They don't know how I manage to look after them all. Well, it's a curious thing, probably borne out by biology, that the more of them there are, the less looking after they need. Indeed, my friends who have only one are exhausted with its care. Those with two are pretty bad; but not as bad as with the one. Those with three find far less than those with two. And so on. A small child has more sense than it is usually credited with. When there is a houseful, they seem instinctively to co-operate."

She studied me shrewdly for a moment.

17

"Look," she said. "You write stories. You take pleasure in creating a story. You must know how poets feel when they create a really great thing. Well, when I discovered I could give life to these beautiful little creatures, I felt the way poets must feel."

Motherhood is the basic creative art.

Gregory Clark

What is a girl?

She is the loudest when you are thinking, the prettiest when she has provoked you, the busiest at bedtime, the quietest when you want to show her off…

Who else can cause you more grief, joy, irritation, satisfaction, embarrassment and genuine delight than this combination of Eve, Salome and Florence Nightingale? She can muss up your home, your hair and your dignity—spend your money, your time and your temper—then, just when your patience is ready to crack, her sunshine peeks through…and you have lost again.

Yes, she is a nerve-wracking nuisance, just a noisy bundle of mischief. But when your dreams tumble down and the world is a mess—when it seems you are pretty much a fool after all—she can make you a king when she climbs on your knee and whispers, "I love you best of all!"

Source unknown

What is a boy?

Boys come in assorted sizes, weights and colours, but all boys have the same creed: to enjoy every second of every minute of every hour of every day and to protest with noise (their only weapon) when their last minute is finished and the adult males pack them off to bed at night.

Boys are found everywhere—on top of, underneath, inside, climbing on, swinging from, running around or jumping to. Mothers love them, little girls hate them, older sisters and brothers tolerate them, adults ignore them and Heaven protects them.

When you are busy, a boy is an inconsiderate, bothersome, intruding jangle of noise.

He likes ice cream...Christmas...comic books...woods...water (in its natural habitat)...large animals...trains...Saturday morning and fire engines. He is not much for Sunday school, company, school, books without pictures, music lessons, neckties, barbers, girls, overcoats, adults or bedtime.

A boy is a magical creature—you can lock him out of your workshop but you cannot lock him out of your heart. You can get him out of your study, but you can't get him out of your mind. Might as well give up—he is your captor, your jailer, your boss, and your master—a freckle faced, pint sized, cat chasing bundle of noise. But when you come home at night with only the shattered pieces of your hopes and dreams, he can mend them like new with two magic words—"Hi, Dad!"

Source unknown

Your kids won't always believe what you say, but they will always believe what you do.

Dan Hare, musician, teacher

CHRISTMAS

Letter to 12 local businesses

Your ad. in the local paper, "Happy Holiday," is cravenly offensive.

There would not be a holiday if it were not for Christmas. People trim their Christmas trees, wish each other a Merry Christmas, exchange Christmas gifts and lots of people even go to church on Christmas Day.

Wake up and face the fact that Christmas is the only reason that there is a holiday in the first place. Do you really think for one split second that Hindus, Sikhs, Moslems and Jews would stop referring to their own feast days for fear of "offending" people? It is a question of mutual respect and "when in Rome…"

Your silly ad is meaningless, nauseating and offensive.

Face the fact that it is the Christmas holiday—Christmas, Christmas, Christmas.

A. Michael Warrington, December 28, 2004

COMMON SENSE

The Death of Common Sense

Common Sense, also known as C.S., lived a long life but died from heart failure at the brink of the millennium. No one really knows how old he was—his birth records were long ago entangled in miles and miles of bureaucrat red tape.

Known affectionately to close friends as Horse Sense and Sound Thinking, he selflessly devoted himself to a life of service in homes, schools, hospitals and offices, helping folks get the job done without a lot of fanfare, whooping and hollering. Rules and regulations and petty, frivolous lawsuits held no power over Common Sense.

A most reliable sage, he was credited with cultivating the ability to know when to come in out of the rain, the discovery that the early bird gets the worm and how to take the bitter with the sweet. C.S. also developed sound financial policies (don't spend more than you earn) reliable parenting strategies (the adult is in charge, not the kid) and prudent dietary plans (offset eggs and bacon with a little fibre and orange juice).

A veteran of the Industrial Revolution, the Great Depression, the Technological Revolution and the Smoking Crusades, C. S. survived sundry, cultural and educational trends including disco, the Men's Movement, body piercing, whole language and New Math.

C.S.' health began declining in the late 1960s when he became infected with the "If-It-Feels-Good, Do-It" virus. In the following decades his waning strength proved no match for the ravages of overbearing Federal and State rules and regulations and an oppressive tax code. C.S. was sapped of strength and the will to live as the Ten Commandments became contraband. Criminals received better treatment than victims, and judges stuck their noses in everything from Boy Scouts to professional baseball and golf.

His deterioration accelerated as schools implemented zero-tolerance policies. Reports of six year old boys charged with sexual harassment for kissing classmates, a teen suspended for taking a swig of Scope mouthwash after lunch, girls suspended for possessing Midol and an honour student expelled for having a table knife in her school lunch were more than his heart could endure.

As the end neared, doctors say C.S. drifted in and out of logic but was kept informed of developments regarding regulations on low-flow toilets and mandatory airbags.

Finally, upon hearing about a government plan to ban inhalers from 14 million asthmatics due to a trace of a pollutant that may be harmful to the environment, C.S. breathed his last.

Services will be at Whispering Pine Cemetery. C.S. was preceded in death by his wife, Discretion, one daughter, Responsibility; and one son, Reason. He is survived by two step-brothers, Half-Wit and Dim-Wit. Memorial contributions may be sent to the Institute for Rational Thought.

Farewell, Common Sense, may you rest in peace.

Lori Borgman, columnist, *Indianapolis Star*, March 15, 1998

COUNSELING

Recent studies in the United States suggest what has been obvious to common sense for many years: that the therapeutic claims of psychotherapy are often unfounded. Talking cures and indulging one's feelings may be worse than useless; grief counselling may actually increase children's distress. Adults appear to benefit from self-discipline, a little old fashioned stoicism and a dignified silence, as Freud himself occasionally suggested.

Minette Marrin writing in the *Sunday Telegraph*, May 16, 1999

COUNTRY AND WESTERN VERSES

Out Where the West Begins

Where the handshake's a little stronger.
Where the sun shines a little longer.
That's where the West begins.

Arthur Chapman (1873–1935), U.S. poet and author

—Perhaps the best known bit of verse in America. It hangs framed in the office of the Secretary of the Interior in Washington. It has been quoted in Congress and printed as campaign material for at least two governors. It has crossed the Atlantic and the Pacific and throughout America it can be found pinned on walls and pasted in innumerable scrapbooks.

Out Among the Big Things

Out among the big things—
The mountains and the plains—

An hour ain't important,
Nor are the hour's gains;
The feller in the city
Is hurried night and day,
But out among the big things
He learns the calmer way.

Out among the big things—
The skies that never end—
To lose a day ain't nothin'
The days are here to spend;
So why not give 'em freely,
Enjoyin' as we go?
I somehow can't help thinkin'
The good Lord means life so.

Out among the big things—
The heights that gleam afar
A feller gets to wonder
What means each distant star;
He may not get an answer,
But somehow, every night
He feels, among the big things,
That everything's all right.

Arthur Chapman, U.S. poet

Ole Faithful

Ole Faithful, we rode the range together
Ole Faithful, in ev'ry kind of weather
When your roundup days are over
There'll be pastures white with clover
For you, Ole Faithful, pal o' mine

Hurry up old fellow
'Cause the moon is yellow tonight
Hurry up old fellow
'Cause the moon is mellow and bright

There's a coyote howling to the moon above
So carry me back to the one I love
Hurry up ole fellow
'Cause we gotta get home tonight

Source Unknown

—Popularized at different times by the "Singing Cowboys" of the '30s
and '40s, including Gene Autry and Roy Rogers.

_____

DIEPPE

By 1942, during the Second World War, Britain had seen a succession
of defeats.

In 1940, the British Expeditionary Force (BEF) had been
defeated in France, then was defeated in Norway, defeated in Greece,
defeated in Crete and very nearly defeated by Rommel in North Africa.

In the spring of 1942, Stalin was demanding of Churchill and
Roosevelt that they should come to the aid of Russia by launching an
immediate second front in Western Europe.

Although the United States was heavily committed to the war
with Japan and was still in an early stage of military build-up, Roosevelt
gave what amounted to an undertaking for a second front in Europe.
The Americans wanted an almost immediate assault in Western Europe
and Roosevelt suggested at least a "sacrifice landing" before the end of
the year.

Churchill agreed with the urgency of the task, but added that
no one could yet be sure whether the operation would prove feasible
so quickly. Therefore Britain could give no promise that it would
actually be undertaken.

The American president was persuaded by his advisors to give
the British an ultimatum: either agree to a Channel crossing in 1942 or
the United States would withdraw its agreement to the idea that
Germany must be defeated before Japan.

The army and navy planners were anxious to find answers to
the problem of capturing a Channel port. Brooke (British Commander,
Imperial General Staff) pressured Churchill, Roosevelt and U.S.

General George Marshall to give up even the idea of a "lodgement" bridgehead in France in 1942, let alone a full scale invasion. When the decision was taken that there would be no second front in Europe in 1942, Churchill visited Russia to tell Stalin in person. There was an angry quarrel with Stalin.

Brooke was finally persuaded to sanction a limited amphibious assault across the Channel, to gain experience for a future invasion and prompt the Germans to withdraw troops from Russia.

Admiral Mountbatten was given permission to make plans in the spring of 1942 for a cross-Channel raid.

Besides restoring some kind of harmony to relations between the United States and Russia and perhaps making the Germans take the threat of a second front seriously, the object of the Dieppe raid was to provide experience in a major amphibious assault against the strongly defended enemy coast. An operation of this kind had never been tried before. A number of questions needed to be answered if an eventual second front was to have the best possible chance.

Would it be better to prepare the way by preliminary bombardment or try for surprise? Could a major, well defended port be seized without damaging it so badly that it would be useless in the critical hours and days of the immediate build-up? Could tanks land in the first wave and could they get across the beaches and seawalls? What new engineering equipment or weapons would be most useful?

These problems had all been looked at in theory. But they had never been tried out in battle against the kind of defences the Germans were known to have along the French coast.

Following Roosevelt's second front declaration, Hitler had been reinforcing the Channel defences in the spring and early summer of 1942. Between March and August, German strength in France, Belgium and Holland increased by nine divisions. Dieppe was itself protected by concrete pillboxes and barbed wire, with high cliffs and gun emplacements overlooking the beach. There were nearly 50 field and coastal guns, plus three anti-aircraft batteries and some anti-tank guns. It was held by troops of the 302nd Infantry Division and there were considerable reserves behind it, notably the 10th Panzer Division at Amiens.

That there were mixed feelings among the higher command there can be little doubt. The British commando raid on St. Nazaire had been a model of heroism, but its toll in casualties had been frightening. Almost 25 percent of the handpicked force was killed and more than half the remainder captured.

The consensus among students of the Dieppe raid is that it was a necessary venture at the time and valuable lessons were definitely learned.

Major General Hamilton Roberts (Divisional Commander, 2nd Canadian Infantry Division) told his men that it would be "a piece of cake." But Dieppe harshly demonstrated weaknesses in the Allied amphibious capability, as well as deficiencies in British intelligence. German numbers and weapon strength were thought to be much smaller than they actually were. A gross mistake was made in underestimating the German fighting soldier and his swiftness to react—he would never be underestimated again.

Two thousand years ago Sun Tzu wrote: "Deception is not enough, the enemy must be confused."

Both principles of war were painfully missing at Dieppe, but were applied brilliantly before D-Day.

A. Michael Warrington

ECCLESIASTES

To every thing there is a season, and a time
to every purpose under the heaven;

A time to be born, and a time to die;
a time to plant, and a time to pluck up
that which is planted;

A time to kill, and a time to heal;
a time to break down, and a time to build up;

A time to weep, and a time to laugh;
a time to mourn, and a time to dance;

A time to cast away stones,
and a time to gather stones together;

A time to embrace,
and a time to refrain from embracing;

A time to get, and a time to lose;
a time to keep, and a time to cast away;

A time to rend, and a time to sew;
a time to keep silence, and a time to speak;

A time to love, and a time to hate;
a time of war, and a time of peace.

Ecclesiastes 3:1–8

––––––––––––––––

EDUCATION

Education is the ability to listen to almost anything without losing your temper or your self confidence.

Robert Frost

––––––––––––––––

ENCOURAGEMENT

In just two days tomorrow will be yesterday.

Source Unknown

––––––––––––––––

Whatever you can do, or dream you can, begin it.
Boldness has genius, power and magic in it.

Goethe

––––––––––––––––

I plan on living forever. So far, so good.

Source Unknown

The people who will be most successful will not be the strongest or the most intelligent, but the ones most adaptable to change.

Frank Ogden "Dr. Tomorrow"

Remember all the best of our past moments,
Forget the rest.

From a poem by **William Allingham**

The vegetarians seem to have forgotten that their practice is unnatural for homo sapiens. Our species has eaten meat for millions of years during our evolution. Perhaps this is why we have outstripped our vegetarian cousins, the apes, in the evolutionary race.

From a letter by **David Roylands**, Welshpool, Montgomeryshire

---

You cannot know the strength of your anchor until you feel the power of the storm.

Source unknown

Not failure, but low aim, is crime.

For an Autograph, **James Russell Lowell** (1819–1891), American poet

---

This too shall pass.

The Bible, quoted by Abraham Lincoln

Ah, but a man's reach should exceed his grasp.
Or what's a heaven for?

Men and Women, **Robert Browning** (1812–1889), English poet

Cheerfulness

A social skill which helps to ease friction and oil the wheels of inter-personal relationships.

Source Unknown

Dr. Clare's prescription:

One, cultivate a passion.
Two, be part of something bigger than yourself.
Three, avoid introspection.
Four, don't resist change.
Five, live for the moment.
Six, audit your happiness.
Seven, play the part and be happy.

Dr. Anthony Clare, St. Patrick's Hospital, Dublin, Eire

Clay lies still but blood's a rover.
Breath's a ware that will not keep.
Up lad: When the journey's over—
There'll be time enough to sleep.

Reveille, **A.E. Housman** (1859–1936), English poet

Life can only be understood backwards.
But is has to be lived forwards.

Søren Kierkegaard (1813–1855) Danish philosopher and theologian

---

Whatever it requires, you do it to get past it. You must avoid piling up this kind of burden in your life.
You must give yourself emotional closure.

Dr. Phil McGraw

We are all born for a purpose—discovering what the purpose is and fulfilling it to the benefit of others, must be our main aim in life.

Editor's Letter, *This England*, summer, 2002

A Sprig of Green

When I walk along sidewalks, every now and then I will see a little bit of greenery.

There only has to be a little crack in the concrete and there may be a sprig of green pushing up—as though there is a life force that cannot be stifled or denied.

The Force of Life—that is so encouraging—no matter how tough things get, some things are tougher than concrete. There is a life force all around us.

Sometimes we may feel enmeshed in problems and some unfortunates are truly wired into misery with problems that seem insurmountable and yet there is always the hope that things may still get better. The proverbial light on the horizon. Something to think about when we see these little sprigs of green pushing up through cracks in the concrete.

A. Michael Warrington

A Donkey As Your Life Coach

Professor Andy Merrifield was chasing a dream when he moved from England to teach at a university in New York City but, as he admitted recently, "Things didn't work out so well; I felt very lost."

So he went to live "somewhere totally antithetical to (New York)," moving into a farmhouse in France's Auvergne region, an area known for its sought-after green lentils from Le Puy. Intending to slow down the pace of his life, he borrowed a friend's donkey and set out on foot through the countryside of southern France.

"When you go slow and travel with a donkey, you have time to think and daydream. Daydreaming is very important in cleansing stuff that is muddling your mind." Like Robert Pirsig in *Zen and the Art of Motorcycle Maintenance*, Merrifield writes about his "journey of the mind" in his first non-academic book, *The Wisdom of Donkeys*.

Walking with Gribouille, his donkey, provided many "pregnant moments of great meditation," he says. "The donkey just stares out into the forest, and you wonder, 'What is the donkey doing?'…and you just go with it." Merrifield also says his donkey taught him the virtue of staying calm when dealing with "tricky situations." Along the way, an agitated horse appeared, "towering over both of us" and blocking their path. Merrifield had no idea what to do, but Gribouille tranquilly walked away in the opposite direction: "Gribouille alone stayed calm, and let the situation wash over him. I had a lot to learn." Donkeys, apparently, are famous for their cool-headedness. They are often "fielded with nervous horses or can become supervisors in halter breaking," explains the author. Donkeys are also intelligent leaders. If a donkey is introduced to a female horse and a foal during weaning, "the foal will often turn to the donkey for support after it has left its mother."

Merrifield began to mimic the donkey disposition. "If you let yourself drift into that donkey world, taking simple strides and slow deep breaths, calm reigns. Things happen with clarity, with simplicity, decisively."

Before setting out with Gribouille, Merrifield researched his subject by visiting an outdoor, mobile donkey clinic in Egypt where Dr. Mohsen Hassan gives free treatment to abused, overworked donkeys. Hassan told him that "local kids treat donkeys worse than bikes, whacking them with wooden batons, pushing and kicking them, sometimes just for the fun of it."

Historically, Egyptians brutalized their donkeys, Merrifield writes, but donkey milk was considered a luxury drink, as well as the secret to eternal youth. "Cleopatra kept a stable of 300 donkeys; each day she bathed in donkey milk, believing it the key to skin health. She was right: donkey milk is full of fatty acids and vitamins A, E, and F…effective for dry, wrinkled skin." Donkey milk soap is sold in France, adds Merrifield.

At the Sidmouth Donkey Sanctuary in Devon, England, Merrifield learned how donkeys internalize pain. "Horses buck up, rear, kick and make a fuss if they're in pain. With a donkey, it's the complete opposite. Hence, it only appears that a donkey feels no pain." A donkey's pain threshold is similar to a human in emotional denial. Merrifield describes how, for too long, he internalized his unhappiness in New York: "It was painful to admit and I didn't admit it quickly." Donkey's psychic needs are very complex, he writes. "A donkey can spend days and days searching for a missing loved one; and if too perplexed by what's happened, by an inexplicable absence, they can go into a deep depression and die of a broken heart."

In Devon, Merrifield met a donkey that visits residents of a retirement home. Lulu is toilet trained to swish her tail when she needs to go. "She knows it is not proper to do it in a living room!" says Jan Aherne, the manager of the sanctuary. Lulu travels with a plastic flexible bucket as a precaution but has never needed it. When she walks through the retirement home, she is "admittedly a curious sight," writes Merrifield, "a shock for a few; others smile bewilderedly, not believing their eyes, laugh and then suddenly start to cry, tears rolling down their cheeks with joy."

"Travelling with a donkey," Merrifield concludes, "is about asking yourself basic questions. Who am I? Where did I come from? Where am I going?" He quotes Robert Louis Stevenson's 1879 book *Travels with a Donkey in the Cervennes*. "We are all travellers in the wilderness of this world… the best that we can find in our travels is an honest friend."

Julia McKinnell, *Maclean's* magazine

EXERCISE

"The only exercise I ever get is acting as pallbearer at the funerals for my friends who exercise."

Winston Churchill, who weighed 3lbs at birth, smoked and drank heavily and died at the ripe old age of 90.

You may not live longer, but at least you will die healthy.

Source Unknown

FAMILY

Money governs the household
That's the usual plan.
Man governs the money
Baby governs the man.
Woman governs the baby
And teaches it how to trot.
And when you come to reckon it up
It's the woman who governs the lot.

Source Unknown

There is always a risk when older people uproot themselves to be near their offspring, that they expect far more than their sons and daughters can provide—with all the will in the world—while losing all their own independent friends and neighbours.

Source Unknown

<u>The Simplest Things</u>

Recently my daughter went with her family to Disney World in Orlando, Florida—wonderful, fun-filled experience, even had a crocodile show.

While they were there, they went to the beach. While everyone was playing around and swimming in the water, our grandson played in the sand. He had found a length of fishing line with a weight on the end. He played with it all afternoon. Despite entreaties from his mother to "Come in because the water's lovely!" he played in the sand all afternoon with his fishing line and weight.

When the family came back to Vancouver, his mother said to him, "What was the best part of the holiday for you?"

Our grandson replied, "When I found the fishing line with the weight on the end."

A. Michael Warrington

The Great Migrator

I am the great migrator,
Migrating to your side of the bed,
I have to be where you are, you see,
Wherever you are, there I'll be,
Wherever you are, there I'll be.

A. Michael Warrington

—To Helen on her birthday, March 7, 2002. Based on: *The Great Pretender*, **The Platters,** 1956

The Story of My Life

Someday I'm going to write
The story of my life
I'll tell about the time we met
And how my heart can't forget
The way you looked that day.

I want the world to know
Life's like a bramble bush
But on that bush I found a rose
And I just had to let you know
I couldn't let you go.

Since then we've travelled far and wide
Had our ups and downs
You took it all in your stride
And filled me full of pride.

There's one thing left to do
Before my story's through
I had to take you for my wife
So the story of my life
Could start and end,
Could start and end with you.

A. Michael Warrington

—For Helen on her birthday, March 7, 2002. Based on: *The Story of My Life*, **Marty Robbins**

_____

My house is a cozy refuge for me and a haven for others.

Source Unknown

_____

One Mother's Day

Mum and Dad were watching TV when Mum said, "I'm tired and it's getting late. I think I'll go to bed."

She went to the kitchen to make sandwiches for next day's lunches, rinsed out the popcorn bowls, took meat out of the freezer for supper the following evening, checked the cereal box levels, filled the sugar container, put spoons and bowls on the table and started the coffee pot for brewing the next morning.

She then put some wet clothes in the dryer, put a load of clothes into the wash, ironed a shirt and secured a loose button.

She picked up the game pieces left on the table and put the telephone book back in the drawer. She watered the plants, emptied a wastebasket and hung up a towel to dry.

She yawned and stretched and headed for the bedroom. She stopped by the desk and wrote a note to the teacher, counted out some cash for the field trip and pulled a textbook out from hiding under the chair.

She signed a birthday card for a friend, addressed and stamped the envelope and wrote a quick note for the grocery store. She put both near her purse.

Mum then creamed her face, put on moisturizer, brushed and flossed her teeth and trimmed her nails.

Dad called out, "I thought you were going to bed."

"I'm on my way," she said.

She put some water into the dog's dish and put the cat outside, then made sure the doors were locked. She looked in on each of the kids and turned out a bedside lamp, hung up a shirt, threw some dirty socks in the hamper and had a brief conversation with the one up still doing homework.

In her own room, she set the alarm, laid out clothing for the next day, straightened up the shoe rack. She added three things to her list of things to do for tomorrow. About that time, Dad turned off the TV and announced to no one in particular, "I'm going to bed."

And he did...without another thought.

Anything extraordinary here????

Wonder why women live longer????

BECAUSE THEY ARE STRONG, MADE FOR THE LONG HAUL...

(All women are special, especially mothers.)

Source Unknown

Young Mother's Quandary—Going Back to Work

Your company can replace you in a heartbeat. Your child can never replace you.

Dr. Laura Schlessinger

Being A Mother

Somebody said it takes about six weeks to get back to normal after you have had a baby. Somebody doesn't know that once you are a mother "normal" is history.

Somebody said you learn how to be a mother by instinct. Somebody never took a three year old shopping.

Somebody said being a mother is boring. Somebody never rode in a car driven by a teenager with a driver's permit.

Somebody said if you are "good" mother, your child will "turn out good." Somebody thinks a child comes with directions and a guarantee.

Somebody said "good" mothers never raise their voices. Somebody never came out the back door just in time to see her child hit a golf ball through the neighbour's kitchen window.

Somebody said you don't need an education to be a mother. Somebody never helped a fourth grader with his math.

Somebody said you can't love the second child as much as you love the first. Somebody doesn't have two children.

Somebody said a mother can find all the answers to her child rearing questions in a book. Somebody never had a child with stuffed beans up his nose or in his ears.

Somebody said the hardest part of being a mother is labour and delivery. Somebody never watch her "baby" get on the bus for the first day of kindergarten or on a plane headed for military "boot camp."

Somebody said a mother can stop worrying after her child gets married. Somebody doesn't know that marriage adds a new son or daughter-in-law to a mother's heart strings.

Somebody said a mother's job is done when her last child leaves home. Not so!!!

Somebody said your mother knows you love her, so you don't need to tell her.

Somebody isn't a mother.

Source Unknown

Mother

After twenty-one years of marriage, my wife wanted me to take another woman out to dinner and a movie. She said, "I love you, but I know this other woman loves you too, and she would love to spend some time with you."

The other woman that my wife wanted me to visit was my MOTHER, who has been a widow for nineteen years. But the demands of my work and my three children had made it possible to visit her only occasionally. That night I called to invite her to go out for dinner and a movie.

"What's wrong, are you well?" she asked. My mother is the type of woman who suspects that a late night call or a surprise invitation is a sign of bad news.

"I thought that it would be pleasant to spend some time with you," I responded. "Just the two of us."

She thought for a moment and then said, "I would like that very much."

That Friday after work, as I drove over to pick her up, I was a bit nervous. When I arrived at her house, I noticed that she, too, seemed a bit nervous about our date. She was waiting in the door with her coat on. She had curled her hair and was wearing the dress that she had worn to celebrate her last wedding anniversary. She smiled from a face that was as radiant as an angel's.

"I told my friends that I was going to go out with my son, and they were impressed," she said, as she got in to the car. "They can't wait to hear about our meeting."

We went to a restaurant that, although not elegant, was very nice and cozy. My mother took my arm as if she were the first lady. After we sat down, I had to read the menu. Her eyes could only read the large print. Halfway through the entrees, I lifted my eyes to see my mum sitting there staring at me. A nostalgic smile was on her face. "It was I who used to have to read the menu when you were small," she said.

"Then it's time that you relax and let me return the favour," I replied.

During the dinner, we had an agreeable conversation—nothing extraordinary but catching up on recent events of each other's life. We talked so much that we missed the movie.

As we arrived at her house later, she said, "I'll go out with you again, but only if you let me invite you." I agreed.

"How was your dinner date?" asked my wife when I got home.

"Very nice. Much more than I could have imagined," I answered.

A few days later my mother died of a massive heart attack. It happened so suddenly that I didn't have a chance to do anything for her. Some time later, I received an envelope with a copy of a restaurant receipt from the same place where mother and I had dined. An attached note said: "I paid this bill in advance. I wasn't sure that I could be there, but nevertheless I paid for two dinners—one for you and the other for your wife. You will never know what that night meant for me. I love you, son."

At that moment I understood the importance of saying, in time, "I love you" and of giving our loved ones the time that they deserve. Nothing in life is more important than your family. Give them the time they deserve, because these things cannot be put off until "some other time."

Source Unknown

It may be the cock that crows, but it is the hen that lays the egg.

Margaret Thatcher

FATE

Appointment in Samarra

There was a merchant in Baghdad who sent his servant to market to buy provisions, and in a little while the servant came back, white and trembling, and said, "Master, just now when I was in the marketplace, I was jostled by a woman in the crowd and when I turned I saw it was Death that jostled me. She looked at me and made a threatening gesture. Now, lend me your horse and I will ride away from this city and avoid my fate. I will go to Samarra and there Death will not find me."

The merchant lent him his horse and the servant mounted it and he dug his spurs in its flanks and as fast as the horse could gallop he went.

Then the merchant went down to the market place and he saw me standing in the crowd and he came to me and said, "Why did you make a threatening gesture to my servant when you saw him this morning?"

"That was not a threatening gesture," I said. "It was only a start of surprise. I was astonished to see him in Baghdad, for I have an appointment with him tonight in Samarra."

W. S. Maughan (1876–1965) novelist and playwright

THE FIBONACCI SERIES

Leonardo Pisano was a 13th century mathematician also known as Fibonacci. He was influential in the introduction of Arabic numerals into European usage. The mathematical curiosity associated with his name, however, is a sequence of numbers called the Fibonacci series. It starts with 0 (zero) and 1 (one). After that, he used this simple rule: Add the last two numbers to get the next number. This produces the series 0, 1, 2, 3, 5, 8, 13, 21, 34, 55, etc.

The Fibonacci series ceased being simply a mathematical curiosity when it was noted that certain numbers in the series are applicable to spiral or whorled structures in nature. The scales on certain pinecones, for example, are arranged in opposing spirals consisting of five and eight scales each.

Even more striking is the growth ratio in the spiral shells of molluscs, such as the chambered nautilus. The snail-shaped spiral, for example, is based on a series of segments proportional to 1, 2, 3, 5, 8, 13, 21, and 34 in consecutive order.

After the number 3, each succeeding number in the Fibonacci series is 1.618 times as large as the preceding number. This ratio—1.618—has been named The Golden Ratio by art historians, who discovered that it represents a proportion that is not only pleasing to the eye but has been used in the composition of many great works of art. The façade of the Parthenon in Athens can be circumscribed by a rectangle with sides almost exactly in the ratio 1:1.618.

Even musical scales are based on Fibonacci numbers.

Ames Diagnostica, Gothenburg, Sweden

FILMS

Making Casablanca

Curtiz, Film Director, produced a classic with Casablanca, but against all odds, one of those odds being himself. Mike Curtiz was Hungarian and his command of English was excellent, but his pronunciation left something to be desired. At one point they were supposed to be shooting in a Moroccan street filled with vendors, a cart, a donkey and a crowd of people. Curtis reviewed the set before starting and said, "It's very nice, but I want a poodle."

The prop man was upset, "Mike, you never told me that. We don't have one."

"Well, get one," Curtis snapped.

"All right." Nervous now, the prop man said, "What size?"

"What size? A big one, a big one!" Curtis turned away in annoyance.

"What colour?" The prop man persisted.

Curtis threw up his hands, "Dark, you idiot! We're photographing in black and white."

"It's going to take about half an hour."

Curtis rolled his eyes, "You think time is nothing? All right, all right!"

We all went back to our dressing rooms, and Mike and I started a game of chess while Bogey kibitzed. In half an hour the prop man poked his head in happily. "I have it now, Mr. Curtis. Will you come and look?"

"Paul, don't touch the pieces. I think I have you mate in three moves." And Mike went out. We went with him so he wouldn't accuse us of cheating, and there on the set was a beautiful black standard poodle. Mike looked bewildered. "What do I want with a dog?"

"You said you wanted a poodle."

"I wanted a poodle in the street," Curtis shouted "A poodle, a poodle of water!!"

"Oh my God, you mean a puddle!"

"Right. A poodle, a puddle—that's what I want, not a goddamn dog!"

Paul Henreid (1908–1992)

—extract from *Ladies Man: An Autobiography* (1984)

<u>Casablanca</u>

Mike Curtiz, Director of Casablanca, was charming to the major stars
but he was just as rude to the smaller players. There was a bit player, a
refugee German aristocrat, a bad actor, who quickly annoyed Mike
Curtiz. Bogart and I were playing chess one day when there was a
knock on the dressing room door and Claude Rains walked in.

"Do you hear that?" Claude asked, nodding towards the open
door.

We could all hear Curtiz screaming at the German actor. "You
stupid son of a b---! Can't you understand English? Can't you do what
I tell you? Don't try to think, you idiot—just listen to me, and don't be
such a ---!"

"Yes," I agreed. "It is rather awful. I ... we think Mike should
learn to control himself."

Very briskly, Claude, who was always a perfect gentleman, said
"We just won't have that kind of behaviour, will we?"

Uneasily, Bogart said, "Well.... no, no, we really shouldn't."

"If Mike is going to act like that," Claude went on "I don't
want to have anything to do with the film. What about you two?
Bogey? Paul?"

Frowning, but impressed by Claude's moral tone, Bogey
agreed. "Absolutely."

"I think," Claude said "we should tell Michael Curtiz right now
that if he raises his voice like that one more time and uses that
disgusting language, we'll walk off the set. Are you with me?"

Bogart stood up "You bet. Come on, Paul, let's do it."

The three of us walked across the set and I asked "Does Curtiz
do this all the time, talk like that?"

"He can be a real son of a b--- to the bit players." Bogey said
"But watch the way he treats us."

He was right. When Curtiz saw us his whole face and manner
changed and he smiled. "Gentlemen! What can I do for you?"

The three of us had decided that since Claude was the oldest,

and it was his idea, he would be the spokesman. "Mike," he said, "Paul and Bogey and I all feel we should have a happy set from the first day to the last. We don't want to hear an ugly word from you to anyone on this stage." His voice hardened. "Not to a grip, a cameraman or even a bit player!" He nodded towards the unfortunate German actor. Curtiz' eyes widened and his jaw dropped but Claude went on relentlessly.

"What we just heard you say to that man was shameful and we are telling you right now, do it again and we three walk off the set!"

"Oh no! No...I...please," Curtiz stammered. Then he collected himself and said, "Please, I promise you it won't happen again, believe me!"

And for the rest of the shooting he was as good as his word—until the last day. They had to shoot the entire film indoors and they used the biggest stage at Warners for the airport scene at the end. To give the illusion of distance, small models of planes were used in the background and midgets were hired to look like men far off. Fog machines gave the final touch, softening everything and making the stage walls and ceiling invisible.

It was an extremely complicated shot because of the camera angles. They had been shooting since early morning, and each time Claude would either miss the marks by a foot or the windshield wiper would be in the wrong place at the wrong time or the fog would be too thick, or they would get out at the wrong mark—a series of small disasters at every take. Each time the fog had to be blown out and new fog brought in and this took at least a half hour. Finally, Claude drove in, hit the marks perfectly, they all got in the right place and a bit player came up, clicked his heels and was supposed to say, "At your service, Mon Capitaine. The plane leaves for Lisbon....." A very short line. He had said it perfectly all day, and now he began the line and froze. The thing every actor dreads happened. He simply forgot what he had to say.

Curtiz had a pencil in his hand. He snapped it in two and screamed "Cut! Cut!" then slammed down the pieces of pencil and let loose. "You..."

Claude looked at me, I looked at Bogey. Then we three turned and walked off while Curtiz, in horror, shouted "No! No, please!"

Very calmly, Claude called back, "We'll see you in a couple of days, Mike."

We passed him and ducked into one of the dressing rooms. Curtiz was frantic. He called the front gate and tried to close down the whole lot while he had people search all over for the three of us. We managed to hide out for two hours, then at 5:30 came back to a chastened, mild director. We re-shot the scene and miracle of miracles—it worked on the first take.

Paul Henreid (1908–1992)

—Extract from *Ladies' Man: An Autobiography* (1984). Henreid was the son of a Viennese Baron and banker. Until 1940, he worked in England on the stage and in films, and in 1940 he emigrated to the United States. His most famous roles were *Now, Voyager* (1942) and *Casablanca* (1943).

Alter Ego

Everyone wants to be like Cary Grant.
Even I want to be like Cary Grant.

Cary Grant

The University of Victoria Film Society

When we lived in Victoria in the 1960s, we used to belong to the University of Victoria Film Society. It was quite unique in that we were able to watch foreign films which did not normally get shown in the usual cinemas. In those days, there was one cinema which didn't have evening shows on Sundays and we actually took over the Oak Bay Theatre, as it then was, for our exclusive use where we showed these films. Afterwards, we would adjourn to somebody's house to critique them. It was unusual and always interesting.

Every now and again I have thought about the University of Victoria Film Society and wondered if it was still going strong. So one day, I phoned Ivor Burrows, one of the chaps who had been one of the main organizers of the Society.

I reached Ivor on the phone. He is still living in Victoria with his wife Doreen. They were also my patients.

Ivor said the University of Victoria Film Society discontinued the showings at the Oak Bay Cinema ("We put it on the map") but the executive of six people continued to each host a dinner once a year so that they attended six dinners a year and they are still doing it. Ivor said he is no longer really that much interested in films, which surprised me, as he is now so very much into "books and music"—he has a couple of thousand records and CDs.

Quite unexpectedly he said, "You were the best diagnostician we ever had. You could put your finger on things without ordering a whole lot of tests and investigations. A genius at sorting things out."

Amazing.

A. Michael Warrington

First Knight

Guinevere: "Milord, doth thee blah, blah, blah...?"
Arthur, in regal voice: "Nope."
Nope?
What up, Sire?

John Armstrong, *Vancouver Sun*, July 7, 1995

—From a review of *First Knight*, a 1995 film with Sean Connery and Richard Gere, regarding the scene which set the alarm bells ringing for the reviewer.

The Third Man

In Italy for 30 years under the Borgias, they had warfare, terror, murder, bloodshed. They produced Michelangelo, Leonardo da Vinci and the Renaissance. In Switzerland they had brotherly love, 500 years of democracy and peace and what did they produce? The Cuckoo Clock.

Orson Welles *The Third Man* (1949). Film based on the novel by Graham Greene.

What's a movie? A series of moments frozen in time by the only time machine ever invented.

David O. Selznick (1902–1965), film producer. From the play *Moonlight and Magnolias* by **Ron Hutchinson**.

FLORENCE NIGHTINGALE

I think one's feelings waste themselves in words;
They ought all to be distilled into actions which bring results.

Apprehension, uncertainty, waiting, expectation, fear of surprise, do a patient more harm than any exertion.

I attribute my success to this—I never gave or took any excuse.

Were there none who were discontented with what they have, the world would never reach anything better.

It may seem a strange principle to enunciate as the very first requirement in a hospital, that it should do the sick no harm.

Florence Nightingale (1820–1910)

—A pioneer in the nursing field, she established herself as a competent nursing administrator during the Crimean War where her insistence on sanitary conditions cut the death rate considerably. She continued to advance the field in her later years, providing better health service and opportunities for women at the same time.

FRIENDSHIP

Many people will walk in and out of your life, but only true friends will leave footprints in your heart.

To handle yourself, use your head. To handle others, use your heart.

Anger is only one letter short of danger.

If someone betrays you once, it is his fault; if he betrays you twice, it is your fault.

Great minds discuss ideas. Average minds discuss events. Small minds discuss people.

He who loses money, loses much. He who loses a friend, loses much more. He who loses faith, loses all.

Beautiful young people are accidents of nature, but beautiful old people are works of art.

Learn from the mistakes of others. You can't live long enough to make them all yourself.

Friends, you and me...you brought another friend...and then there were three...we started our group...our circle of friends...and like that circle...there is no beginning or end...

Eleanor Roosevelt (1884–1962), wife of Franklin D. Roosevelt, U.S. president (1932–1945)

Make new friends
But keep the old
For one is silver
The other gold.

Source Unknown

GETTING OLDER

Now that he is 78 and living on a maple farm in Caledon, Ontario, Norman Jewison is far from retired, with a couple of projects on the go.

"I hate being old. So I decided I wouldn't buy into it. No shuffling, no complaining about aches and pains. No struggling to remember. No afternoon naps. Just keep working. laughing, drinking and appreciating every smell, sound, taste and touch that one can possibly experience."

Words to live by.

Norman Jewison, maker of films, including *Fiddler on the Roof* and *Jesus Christ Superstar*

It's a question of mind over matter. If you don't mind, it doesn't matter.

Jack Benny

It has been said that time may be a great healer, but it's a lousy beautician.

Source Unknown

Of all the things that you wear
The most important is your expression.

Source Unknown

Resolve to accept your limitations as they appear. If you can do this, you can live a useful and interesting life within them. If you spend all of your time worrying about what you cannot or may not be able to do, you will be a pain in the neck to yourself and everyone else. Also, foster your relationships. Good relationships are essential to a happy life. Does it work? Well, I am a contented 90.

Stan P. Meadows, Soccer player, Manchester, England

Age doesn't always bring wisdom,
Sometimes it comes alone.
Life not only begins at forty, it also begins to show.

Source Unknown

On Getting Older

I am now, probably for the first time in my life, the person I have always wanted to be. Oh, not my body! I sometimes despair over my body, the wrinkles, the bags under the eyes, and the sagging bottom. And often I am taken aback by that old person that lives in my mirror, but I don't agonize over those things for very long.

I would never trade my amazing friends, my wonderful life, my loving family for less grey hair or a flatter abdomen. As I have aged, I have become more kind to myself and less critical of myself. I have become my own friend. I don't chide myself for eating that extra cookie or that piece of chocolate, or for not buying that silly gizmo that I don't really need but looks so avant garde on my patio. I feel I am entitled to a treat, to be a little untidy, to be extravagant.

I have seen too many dear friends leave this world too soon…, before they had a chance to understand the great freedom that comes with aging.

Whose business is it if I chose to read or play around on the computer till 4:00 a.m. and sleep till noon?

I can sometimes dance by myself to those wonderful tunes of the '60s and '70s, walk the beach in swimming trunks, regardless of my aging bod, even though there may be a few pitying glances from the younger set. They, too, will get old in time.

I know I am sometimes forgetful. But there again, some of life is just as well forgotten and I eventually remember the important things. Sure, over the years there have been sadnesses and my heart has been broken. How can your heart not break when you lose a loved one or when a child suffers. But broken hearts are what give us strength, understanding and compassion.

I am so blessed to have lived long enough to have my hair turn grey and to have my youthful laughs forever etched into the deep grooves on my face. So many have never laughed and so many have died before their hair could turn silver.

As you get older, it is easier to be positive. You care less about what other people think. I don't question myself anymore. I've even earned the right to be wrong.

So, to answer your question, I like being old. It has set me free. I like the person I have become. I am not going to live forever but while I am still here I will not waste time lamenting what one could have been or worrying about what will be. And I shall eat ice cream and chocolate every single day—IF I FEEL LIKE IT.

Source Unknown

GLOBALIZATION

An Empire of quite another sort is stealthily and subtly returning to the centre stage. There is a feeling that this new entity is possibly going to exert an unacceptable and undesirable influence over the world. This phenomenon has been referred to as globalization. The old system of un-elected Governors and Viceroys and District Commissioners have all passed away and what has replaced them is an unstructured kind of imperium, with a slew of new and similarly un-elected rulers, which in this case, are banks, corporations and brands, all operating without restriction in a new and economically borderless world. And, on the other hand, a vast and disparate body of subject peoples who are increasingly bound to make use of these banks, corporations and brands and are kept enthralled to them unwittingly, but firmly kept there nonetheless.

The benefits of globalization are proclaimed vociferously by the banks and corporations who are its prime beneficiaries: economies of scale mean that consumer products become cheaper and more widely available; bureaucracy crumbles in the face of corporate-directed efficiency; access to goods and services is more widespread, more democratic; the standard of living everywhere improves—everyone floats higher on an ever-rising tide of global prosperity.

But the darker side of this phenomenon, less readily seen, is what worries many. That the world is becoming increasingly ordered by unelected and faceless figures in distant (and most commonly American) corporate headquarters, figures who are answerable only to the shareholders in the company which is their base of power. There are fewer and fewer controls on those global operators—for under whose law do they operate?—to limit unscrupulous and inhumane behaviour. That the less powerful—the employee in a Third World nation, working under contract for some distant American company whose responsibility is limited by distance and by adroit corporate lawyers—can be oppressed and cheated and denied rights, without anyone to notice or complain. That indigenous businesses can so easily be forced under, unable to stand the competition from the corporate super-giants, whose growing share of world trade seems unstoppable and whose ruthlessness is glorified by managers, who see it as an essential for success.

Simon Winchester, *Outposts (Journeys to the Surviving Relics of the British Empire)*, 1985

HAPPINESS AND CONTENTMENT

<u>Making a Difference</u>

"What does a snowflake weigh?"
"Nothing."
"Oh, come on. It must weigh something."
"Well, next to nothing, almost nothing."
"Well, picture a branch on a tree, bent under a huge collection of snow and a few snowflakes are still falling. Then, suddenly, one last snowflake weighing—what did you say?—next to nothing?—and the branch breaks. That one snowflake made the difference."

Source unknown

It is definitely my sort of car—supremely comfortable to drive 300 miles non-stop, with a delightful gear box and enough acceleration to make life interesting.

I take my driving very seriously. When I get into the Jaguar, I feel relaxed and exhilarated at the same time. A unique experience.

Nigel Clarke, AA Operations Director, *Sunday Times*, June 19, 1988

_____

Making a movie is like writing "War and Peace" in a bumper car in an amusement park and there are few greater pleasures than when it all comes together.

Stanley Kubrick (1928–1999) film director

_____

If you're always wanting something else or something more,
You will miss the happiness behind your own front door.
All you need for heart's content can be created there.
Heaven's where you make it—all around you, everywhere.

Source Unknown

_____

Tomorrow is a landscape that is hidden from your view, so waste no time in wondering what it will hold for you.
Take what life now offers with a quiet and thankful mind,
In your own small corner many small treasures you will find.

Source Unknown

_____

Don't despise contentment, it is something rich and rare,
In an age of restlessness, frustration and despair.
It is an achievement: in itself a victory,
To make a world within a world—and live contentedly.

Source Unknown

_____

Me and my Jag

Contentment is not the fulfilment of what you want but the realization of how much you already have.

Source Unknown

Salud Y Pesetas Y Tiempo Para Gastarlos.
Translation: Health and dollars and the time to spend them.

Mgr. Michael Lee

The writer, William Saroyan, once said that he knew everyone had to die but that he hoped an exception might be made in his case. I would go along with that.

Miriam Margolyes, actress

Tucked away in our subconscious minds is an idyllic vision. We see ourselves on a long, long trip…we are travelling by passenger train and out the windows we drink in the passing scene…cars on nearby highways…cattle grazing on a distant hillside…row upon row of corn and wheat…flatlands and valleys of mountains and rolling hillsides…

But uppermost in our minds is the final destination...and once we get there so many wonderful dreams will come true…restlessly we pace the aisles waiting, waiting, waiting for the station.

However, sooner or later we must realize there is no one station, no one place to arrive at once and for all. The true joy of life is the trip. The station is only a dream. It constantly outdistances us.

"When we reach the station, that will be it!" we cry. Translated it means, "When I am 18, that will be it! When I buy a new 450 Mercedes Benz, that will be it! When I put the last kid through college that will be it! When I have paid off the mortgage, that will be it! When I win a promotion that will be it! When I reach the age of retirement, that will be it! I shall live happily ever after!"

Unfortunately, once we get "it" then "it" disappears. The station somehow hides itself at the end of an endless track.

"Relish the moment" is a good motto…It isn't the burdens of today that drive men mad. Rather, it is regret over yesterday or fear of tomorrow. Regret and fear are twin thieves who would rob us of today.

So, stop pacing the aisles and counting the miles. Instead, climb more mountains, eat more ice cream, go bare foot oftener, swim more rivers, watch more sunsets, laugh more and cry less. Life must be lived as we go along. The station will come soon enough.

Robert J. Hastings writing in the *Illinois Baptist*

… so, the most restless vagabond finally yearns to return to his native land and find in his little cottage, on the breast of his wife, in the circle of his children, in the business of supporting them, the bliss which he sought in vain in the big world!

Goethe, from *The Sorrows of Young Werther*

Health is the greatest possession. Contentment is the greatest treasure. Confidence is the greatest friend.

Lao Tzu, 6th Century BC Chinese philosopher

HEALTH NOTES

Research is increasingly showing that a person can reap the potential health benefits of antioxidant intake by eating a diet rich in antioxidant-containing foods. As a bonus, foods high in antioxidants typically offer many other health benefits as well.

Antioxidants are thought to be helpful because they can neutralize free-radicals which are toxic by-products of natural cell metabolism. Free radicals can also be introduced into the body by exposure to certain substances such as cigarette smoke or pesticides.

One reason why foods appear to be a better choice than taking oral supplements is that foods contain an unmatchable array of antioxidant substances. A supplement may contain a single type of antioxidant—or even several. However, foods contain thousands of types of antioxidants—Vitamin A alone has several hundred forms—and it's not known which of these substances are able to confer benefits. In fact, researchers theorize that antioxidants in food form chemical networks that then interact with our own cellular and genetic intricacies.

In addition, although supplements containing antioxidants are generally considered safe, two recent studies have suggested that taking higher doses of supplements such as Vitamin E over time may actually increase a person's risk of death.

In contrast, foods higher in antioxidants are often plant-based and offer health benefits in addition to their antioxidant content, such as being high in fibre, protein and other vitamins and minerals and low in saturated fat and cholesterol.

When it comes to antioxidant intake, no one food or food group should be your sole focus. It is best to include a wide variety of foods from the categories listed below as part of a healthy, well-balanced diet. Some of the better sources of anti-oxidants include:

Berries—Blueberries, blackberries, raspberries, strawberries and cranberries are among the top sources of antioxidants.

Beans—Small red beans and kidney, pinto and black beans are among the top sources of antioxidants.

Fruits—Many apple varieties (with peel) are high in antioxidants, as are avocadoes, cherries, green and red pears, fresh or dried plums, pineapple, oranges, kiwi and others.

Vegetables—Those with the highest antioxidant content include artichokes, spinach, red cabbage, red and white potatoes (with peel), sweet potatoes and broccoli. Although the effect of cooking on antioxidant levels varies by cooking method and vegetable, one recent study showed that cooking generally increased levels among select vegetables.

Beverages—Green tea may come to mind as a good source of antioxidants but other beverages have high levels too, including coffee, red wine and many fruit juices.

Nuts—Walnuts, pistachios, pecans, hazelnuts and almonds are some of the top nuts for antioxidant content.

Herbs—These may be unexpected suppliers of antioxidants but ground cloves, cinnamon, or ginger, dried oregano leaf and turmeric powder are all good sources.

Grains—In general, oat-based products are higher in antioxidants than those that are derived from other grain sources.

Dark Chocolate—A piece of dark chocolate ranks as high or higher than most fruits and vegetables in terms of antioxidant content.

Extract from *Mayo Clinic Health Letter*, September, 2007

HIGH FLIGHT

Oh! I have slipped the surly bonds of earth
And danced the skies on laughter-silvered wings;
Sunward I've climbed,
and joined the tumbling mirth
Of sun-split clouds,
—and done a hundred things
You have not dreamed of—
wheeled and soared and swung
High in the sunlit silence,
Hov'ring there,
I've chased the shouting wind along,
and flung
My eager craft through
footless halls of air...
Up, up the long delirious, burning blue,
I've topped the wind-swept heights
with easy grace
Where never lark, or even eagle flew –
And, while with silent, lifting mind
I've trod
The high untrespassed sanctity of space,
Put out my hand and touched the face of God.

John Magee (1922–1941)**,** Pilot Officer**,** No. 412 Squadron RCAF

John Magee, aged 16, showing his mother the letter telling
him of winning the school's Poetry Prize

John Magee receives his all-important "Wings" in 1941

—John Magee was born in Shanghai in 1922, the eldest of four boys. (His English mother had gone to China as a CMS missionary in 1919, and there she met and married an American Episcopalian, the Rev. John Magee.) At the age of nine, young John was sent to an English boarding school in Kent, and later attended Rugby Public School.

In 1939, John's father was still in China, but his mother and his brothers had returned to England to live near Dover in Kent. John was persuaded to go to America (at first rather against his wishes), where he finished high school near Hartford, Connecticut prior to going to Yale (where his father had graduated). He was homesick for England and wrote to his mother: "I shall never be really happy here. I am convinced that my place is in England...."

By the spring of 1940, he was becoming increasingly restless. But on trying to enlist in the RAF, the American State Department refused the necessary visa. He decided to go to Ottawa and join the RCAF. He trained as a pilot and was posted to England, where he flew operations in a Spitfire fighter squadron.

He was killed in a flying accident in December, 1941, at the age of 19.

A War Time Collision

A few years ago while on holiday... I noticed a poem in the Armstrong Museum at Bamburgh Castle. It was the famous "High Flight" by John Magee. I was fascinated by the poem because it summed up my feelings at the time when I had been a Flight Cadet at RAF College, Cranwell, Lincolnshire, in 1941.

I took a note of the publishers of the book in which the poem was printed (This England) and later sent for a copy of the book. I was astonished to read Stephen Garnett's biography of John Magee. I discovered for the first time that he and my best friend at Cranwell, Aubrey Griffin, died together in a mid-air collision. John Magee's Spitfire and Aubrey Griffin's Oxford Trainer.

Apparently a flight of Spitfires from RAF Digby (where John Magee was based) had been scrambled to intercept an enemy intruder.

RAF Digby was close to the satellite airfield at Barkston where at this crucial time Aubrey was practising circuits in his Oxford.

According to eyewitnesses, the first two Spitfires narrowly

THE SUPERMARINE SPITFIRE

missed the Oxford Trainer as they hurriedly climbed in pursuit of the intruder, but the third one went straight into the Oxford, causing it to virtually explode.

The Spitfire pilot managed to bail out, but unfortunately his parachute opened a fraction too late and he died in the ambulance later.

So, without firing a shot, that enemy plane had caused the death of two pilots and the destruction of their aircraft.

Ronald Holton, Gifford, East Lothian, letter to *This England*, Spring, 2001

HISTORY

It is interesting to speculate what India would be like now if it had not had the "benefit" of the influence of the British Empire.

H. Norcross, Farnham Royal, Bucks, letter to the *Sunday Telegraph*

<u>As It Was</u>

The world has changed a great deal since I (AMW) was a boy growing up in England. As Simon Winchester said:

There were once a number of Empires—French, German, Dutch, Portuguese, Spanish and the British. It can be said that the British Empire managed to leave behind a kind of legacy of which, dare one say it, some might still be rightly proud.

The Empire stretched over one-quarter of the land surface of the globe and included one-quarter of the world's population. Over this Empire, Queen Victoria reigned with supposed benevolence and wisdom. Great nation-states, or nations in the making—India, Canada, Australia, South Africa—were governed from Whitehall by her servants and in her name.

Nowadays, one might question whether these "possessions" were left better off than if the British had never come. That there were abuses and suppression is beyond doubt.

Was the end result all that bad?

Hong Kong, since 1997, once again a part of China, offers an example of that legacy. There is a system of democracy in place, imperfect perhaps, and offered to the citizens very late in their territory's history, but which is somewhat more accountable than the cruel apparatus of government imposed by Beijing. There are courts that are, by and large, fair and impartial. Business contracts are exchanged and honoured by all parties. The police force is much respected and little feared. There is a bureaucracy made up of talented civil servants, its senior managers are generally free from corruption. The press is vocal, colourful and still more or less free to write and say what it likes. There are several good universities. A system of primary and secondary education open to all. A cadre of teachers of impeccable training and talent. The postal system works faultlessly. The railway system is the envy of the world. The environment is moderately well protected. The arts are reasonably well assisted—Hong Kong is, in short, a part of China in which any civilized human might wish to live. It might be said that even the most anti-Colonial campaigner might be able to acknowledge that the essential liveable decency of the place stems not necessarily from any peculiarly innate goodness in the people, but from—may one dare say this today ?—the wisdom and benevolence of the Colonial masters who planned and ruled that territory for the century and a half so lately ended.

Much the same might be said of a whole raft of former British possessions. Comparisons between the practical aspects of living in almost any one of them and of living in countries once ruled by rival Empires, nearly always tend to favour which ever one was once directed from London.

Compare, for example, the courts in (formerly British-run) Malaysia with those in Indonesia, where the Dutch so long held sway. Post a domestically bound letter in a village outside Bombay and compare its progress with one similarly mailed in a town near Tijuana. The railway system in Kenya (British) still works splendidly; that in Ethiopia (as Abyssinia, Italian) is dire. Papeete (French) is a tawdry Tahitian slum. Apia (once British, as Samoa) is a quiet mid-Pacific gem. And so on and so on.

So there is perhaps some justification for an affection for the relics of the British Empire.

A visitor to the few remaining outposts may feel a certain sense of pride when such previous Colonial subjects as remain talk of their lingering links with far away London.

India was left with a thriving democratic form of government, a modern communications network, a comprehensive rail and road network, a fair judicial service, a full education and hospital system and a mainly corruption-free and efficient civil service by the British.

Simon Winchester, *Outposts* (1985)

———————————

They had made up their mind that they were going to go to war. I believe to this day, and I always have, and I have said so publicly many times in regretting my vote, that there was a pre-determination.

Congress would not have authorized that war if we knew what we know now.

Tragically, the intelligence failures set out in this report will affect our National Security for generations to come. Our credibility is diminished. Our standing in the world has never been lower. We have fostered a deep hatred of Americans in the Muslim world, and that will grow. As a direct consequence, our Nation is more vulnerable today than ever before.

Senator John Rockefeller

—Democratic senator from West Virginia, commenting on the U.S. invasion of Iraq. Senate 517-page Investigative Report, July, 2004.

———————————

HOLLYWOOD

You can take all the sincerity in Hollywood, place it in a flea's navel and still have enough room for six caraway seeds and an agent's heart.

Quoted by **Jack Paar**, *Tonight Show* host (1957–1962)

———————————

Hollywood is a place where they pay you one thousand dollars for a kiss and fifty cents for your soul.

Marilyn Monroe (1926–1962)

HUMOUR

Utah greeting card:

In Utah, a Man marries a Woman—
And a Woman, and a Woman and a Woman.

Anonymous anaesthetist

<u>Getting the Point Across</u>

When Benjamin Disraeli was called to order for declaring half the Cabinet were asses. "Mr. Speaker, I withdraw," he apologized, "half of the Cabinet are not asses."

Benjamin Disraeli, 19th century Conservative Prime Minister

Wry Argentineans used to call themselves "A race of Italians, who speak Spanish, act like the French and wish we were English."

Source Unknown

Two bald men fighting over a comb.

Jorge Luis Borges (1899–1986), Argentine poet and writer

—Condemning the Falklands War, 1982

Depends How You Look at Things

Patient: What—Two hundred dollars just for putting me to sleep?
Anaesthetist: No—Two hundred dollars for making sure you wake up!

Source Unknown

We are here on Earth to do good for others. What the others are here for, I don't know.

W.H. Auden English poet (1907–1973)

Britain is Repossessing the USA

To: The Citizens of the United States of America
    In light of your failure to nominate competent candidates for President of the USA and thus to govern yourselves, we hereby give notice of the revocation of your independence, effective immediately.
    Her Sovereign Majesty Queen Elizabeth II will resume monarchical duties over all States, Commonwealth and Territories (except Kansas, which she does not particularly care for). Your new Prime Minister, Gordon Brown, will appoint a Governor for America without the need for further elections.
    Congress and the Senate will be disbanded.
    A questionnaire may be circulated next year to determine whether any of you had noticed.
    To aid in the transition to a British Crown Dependency the following rules are introduced to take effect immediately:
    You should look up "revocation" in the Oxford English Dictionary. Then look up aluminium and check the pronunciation guide. You will be amazed at just how wrongly you have been pronouncing it.
    The letter "u" will be reinstated in words such as favour, neighbour. Also, you will learn to spell donut without skipping half the letters and the suffix "ize" will be replaced by the suffix "ise." Generally, you will be expected to raise your vocabulary to acceptable levels. (Look up vocabulary)

Using the same 27 words interspersed with filler noises, such as "like" and "you know," is an unacceptable and inefficient form of communication. There is no such thing as "U.S. English." We will let Microsoft know on your behalf. The Microsoft spellchecker will be adjusted to take account of the reinstated letter "u" and the elimination of "ize." You will relearn your original National Anthem, God Save the Queen.

July the 4th will no longer be celebrated as a holiday.

You will learn to resolve personal issues without using guns, lawyers or therapists. The fact that you need so many lawyers and therapists shows that you are not adult enough to be independent.

Guns should only by handled by adults. If you are not adult enough to sort things out without suing someone or speaking to a therapist, then you are not grown up enough to handle a gun.

Therefore, you will no longer be allowed to own or carry anything more dangerous than a vegetable peeler. A permit will be required if you wish to carry a vegetable peeler in public.

All American cars are hereby banned. This is for your own good. When we show you German cars, you will know what we mean.

All intersections will be replaced with roundabouts and you will start driving on the left hand side with immediate effect. This will help you to understand the British sense of humour.

You will learn to make real chips. The things you call french fries are not real chips and the things you insist on calling potato chips are properly called crisps. Real chips are thick cut, fried in fat and dressed not with ketchup but with vinegar.

Hollywood will be required to cast English actors as the good guys. Hollywood will also be required to cast English actors to play English characters.

Watching Andie McDowell attempt to speak with an English accent in Four Weddings and a Funeral was an experience akin to having a haircut with a cheese grater.

You will stop playing American football. There is only one kind of proper football, it is called soccer. Those of you brave enough will, in time, be allowed to play rugby (which has some similarities to American football, but does not involve stopping for a rest every 20 seconds or wearing full body armour).

Furthermore, you will stop playing baseball. It is not reasonable to host an event called the World Series for a game which is not played outside America. Since only two percent of you are aware that there is a world beyond your borders, your error is understandable. You will learn cricket.

An internal revenue agent (i.e. tax collector) from Her Majesty's Government will be with you shortly to ensure the acquisition of all monies due (backdated to 1776).

Daily tea time begins promptly at 4:00 p.m. with proper cups, never mugs, high quality biscuits (cookies) and cakes.

God Save the Queen.

John Cleese, British comedian

If this is coffee, please bring me some tea. If this is tea, please bring me some coffee.

Abraham Lincoln

IMPARTING KNOWLEDGE

My son, more than the calf wishes to suck does the cow yearn to suckle?

Rabbi Akiba (in Roman captivity) to his favourite pupil Simeon ben Yochai

---

INSPIRATION

A visit to Mother Theresa

When I finally met Mother Theresa, I discovered she was very tiny— less than five feet tall—and kept her head cocked to one side. She had gnarled hands and thick peasant feet that protruded from under her coarse white sari with its distinctive blue trim. Although there was no mistaking the aura of the warmth and kindness that surrounded her, I felt I was in the presence of the most powerful, focused and determined person I had ever met. As we chatted, she held my hands in hers and her eyes, kind yet fiercely intense, never left mine. She talked about her 400 homes throughout the world and about the work.

Nancy Lockhart writing in the *Globe and Mail*, September, 1997

————————

She was tall and fair and lovely, her eyes large and clear, her hair like wind amongst the wheat. She came back from vacation and hugged her kids in public and we knew, we just knew, she must be a good mother. There really was a person named Diana. And there was the Diana people loved.

Editorial, Globe and Mail, September 6, 1997

————————

Smile

A smile creates happiness in the home, fosters goodwill in business and is the counter-sign to friends.
It is rest to the weary, daylight to the discouraged, sunshine to the sad and nature's best antidote for trouble.
Yet it cannot be bought, begged, borrowed or stolen; for it is something that is of no earthly good to anyone until it is given away.
And if someone is too tired to give you a smile, just give them one of yours.
For nobody needs a smile as much as those who have none left to give.

Source Unknown

————————

Interview with Dr. Marshall Dahl

BCMJ: You have also mentioned that you enjoy working in the ER and ICU. Can you tell me about that?
Dr. Dahl: I enjoy those environments because they are microcosms of why I got into medicine. You are treating people who are quite sick, they need help now, so you can make a difference. It is very stimulating because these are complicated cases, with many interacting problems. I

like solving problems, but ultimately, I like problems that mean something when you are finished. And, I really like the people who work in emergency rooms, particularly emergency room nurses and ICU nurses—they are focused, sharp and have great personalities.

BC *Medical Journal*, September, 2000

AN IRISH TOAST

My mother came from Galway in Ireland. On festive occasions when we had a glass of wine at home or a glass of sherry, my mother would raise her glass and say, *Sláinte go saol agat*, an Irish toast. I never knew the exact translation.

A few years ago we were visiting Dublin and we were invited out to have dinner with a Professor of Gaelic Studies. I asked him about the spelling and pronunciation of *Sláinte go saol agat* and he said, "I've never heard of it."

Recently I came across the exact spelling and translation and here it is:

Sláinte go saol agat, translated from Gaelic means "Health for life to you."

A. Michael Warrington

LANGUAGE

German is the language to speak to dogs.
English is the language to speak to horses.
Italian is the language to speak to men.
French is the language to speak to women.
But Spanish…Ahhh, Spanish is the language to speak to God!

Paul Stocklin, former patient of AMW

—Stocklin, an accountant originally from Switzerland, was sitting on a park bench in Retiro Park, Madrid in May, 1923 studying Spanish from a book.

A priest sitting nearby said, "I see you are learning Spanish—do you like Spanish?"

Paul said, "Yes—I already speak French, Italian and German and I would like to learn Spanish."

The priest said, "Spanish is a beautiful language." Then he quoted the above, blessed Paul and walked away.

LAW

If we are not to be governed by laws which reflect the deepest beliefs of the majority, what are we to be governed by?

Lynette Burrows, writing in the *Sunday Telegraph*, October, 1995

Don't jump until you get to the stile.

Old legal maxim as quoted in *Rumpole and the Primrose Path*, **John Mortimer**

It Depends What You Mean By...

Members of the medical profession play an important role in litigation. In most cases where damages are claimed for personal injury, they can be seen on the plaintiff's side giving forceful evidence of permanent disability resulting from the injury and, on the defendant's side, of complete and absolute recovery.

Years ago in Dublin, Dr. Arthur Chance, an orthopaedic surgeon, was very sought after by insurance companies. He was strikingly handsome with silver hair, silver moustache, immaculate blue pin-striped suit and he consulted his notes with the aid of a monocle. A counsel appearing for the employer in a Workman's Compensation case might get five guineas, but it was said that Dr. Chance got 100 guineas, and a car to bring him to the courthouse. On one occasion he went to a town in County Tipperary, instructed by an insurance company. The case was a Workman's Compensation review. The man's employer thought he had recovered sufficiently to return to work.

Taking the oath, Dr. Chance consulted his notes, "This man, age 35, told me that he hurt his back by lifting a bale of straw two years ago. I examined him thoroughly, during the course of which he said he was no better—the pain was terrible. I remember asking him to bend forward and he winced in pain. Asked to touch his toes, he couldn't get his hands even near his knees. When I palpated his back, he jumped in agony and asked me to stop.

However, I had asked him to undress for the examination and although he didn't know it, I observed him closely. To take off his trousers, he had to bend down to remove the trousers as he still had his shoes on. His back movements during this were free and perfect. The same applied when he dressed again."

"What was your conclusion?" asked the judge.

"In my opinion, this man has completely recovered and no objective reason can be found for his pain. On undressing and dressing, all movements of his back were full and painless."

The employer's barrister beamed and sat down. The insurance man in the back of the court gave a smirk.

The workman's counsel stood up.

"I'm calling his local general practitioner, My Lord."

There could not have been a greater contrast between the dapper Dr. Chance and the local doctor with his dishevelled suit, untidy hair, stained tie and strong rustic accent.

"What," asked the judge, "is your opinion of the applicant?"

"I know this man well. He cannot work. He has got a bad back. He is a genuine character and an honest man. It's my own view he will never again be fit for labouring work."

"What did you find wrong with him?"

"Ah, he must have strained his back, the weight was too much. All his muscles and vertebrae are sore. I know all his family and they are all genuine. Workers to a man and woman. He was a rare fellow until he got this injury."

The employer's counsel got up to cross-examine him.

"You say he hurt his back. What muscle did he strain?"

73

"Ah, one of those muscles that's attached to the spine. The lumbar muscle, they're all over the back."

"Didn't you say on one occasion, the last time we were here, that he had a pain in his neck?"

"Sure," said the doctor, "he had. It was all over his back, everywhere."

"Did you pay attention to Dr. Chance's evidence?"

"I did."

"You heard Dr. Chance say"—dramatic pause—"that he could undress himself without pain, managing his trousers, both dressing and undressing. Have you any comment to make about that?"

"Yes."

"Well, what do you say?"

"Now," said the doctor, "he won't get any work in this town bending down and pulling up his trousers."

The man's compensation was not cut off, and he and his doctor went happily to the nearest pub.

Irish Days, Memoirs of Judge **Patrick Mackenzie**

Thickets of the Law

Roper: So now you would give the Devil benefit of law!

More: Yes. What would you do? Cut a great road through the law to get after the Devil?

Roper: I'd cut down every law in England to do that!

More: Oh? And when the last law was down and the Devil turned around on you—where would you hide, Roper, the laws all being flat? This country's planted thick with laws from coast to coast—man's laws, not God's—and if you cut them down... do you really think you could stand upright in the winds that would blow then? Yes, I'd give the Devil benefit of the law, for my own safety's sake.

Exchange between Sir Thomas More and his son-in-law, William Roper, in **Robert Bolt**'s play, *A Man For All Seasons*

LETTERS TO THE EDITOR

The pro-abortion lobby maintains that a foetus is not human and the choice of the mother to terminate is, thus, paramount. The anti-abortionist argument is that a foetus is a human being and killing it is, therefore, wrong. As a former foetus, I support the latter view.

Sunday Telegraph, **C.W.R. Cooke**, Little Chalfont, August 17, 2003

We are all born for a purpose—discovering what that purpose is and fulfilling it to the benefit of others must be our main aim in life.

Editor's letter, *This England*, summer, 2002

The Original Desert Rat

C.N.R. Stewart (letter—August 24th) is mistaken in stating that the Desert Rat applied originally and exclusively to the besieged Tobruk Garrison in 1941.

The Desert Rat was the emblem of the famous Seventh Armoured Division. The Division's background was the Western Desert, some of the regiments having been in Egypt since 1936, tasked with the defence of Egypt and the Suez Canal against the threat of Italian aggression. The men of the Division were called Desert Rats after the jerboa, the hardy little denizen of the inhospitable desert said to have remarkable powers of speed and survival. The Divisional emblem was born in 1940. The Divisional Commander's wife (Mrs. Creagh) went to the Cairo Zoo and produced a sketch on a sheet of hotel notepaper, a Desert Rat. This was transferred, in flaming scarlet, to the Divisional flag and thence, on to every vehicle in the Division.

The Seventh Armoured Division was the first to engage the Italians in battle in June, 1940. They fought Erwin Rommel (The Desert Fox) across North Africa, into Italy and Normandy (landing on D-Day plus one), Belgium, Holland and finally Germany, "a march unsurpassed through all the story of war..." (Winston Churchill, Victory Parade, Berlin, 1945).

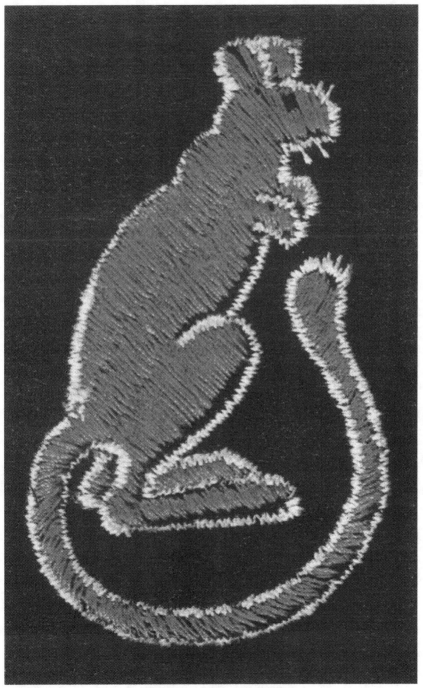

The Jerboa, "Desert Rat"

I was a Tank Troop Leader in the Seventh Armoured Division in Normandy and I still have my shoulder flashes, which have a red jerboa on a black background.

The German description of the Tobruk Garrison like "rats in the trap" may have been apt, though hardly flattering, but the original Desert Rats they were not.

A. Michael Warrington, Tsawwassen, BC

—Letter to the Editor, *Globe and Mail*, August 28, 1996

Dear Sir or Madam:

The unflattering bit of cowardly sniping at Field Marshal Montgomery, undeservedly described as a character sketch, which Christopher Hibbert (May 28) attributes to Peter Paterson, reflects poorly on those two gentlemen and will certainly not tarnish the memory of one of Britain's greatest generals.

Yours sincerely, **A. Michael Warrington**

—*Sunday Times Books*, July 5, 1989

Don't Blame Oldsters

Every generation has challenges to meet and thinks times are tough like never before.

Having endured the Depression of the 1930s, the Second World War, the inflationary 1970s and successive spend thrift governments—starting with Trudeau—the older generations are now being blamed for the debt.

It's not the oldies who created Canada's debt, but irresponsible politicians of every political stripe—and they are still doing it—pouring money into idiotic projects and all too often into the pockets of corrupt Third World politicians under the label "foreign aid," being just two examples among many.

A. Michael Warrington, Tsawwassen, BC

—Letter to *Financial Post*, January 6, 1995, in response to the article: "Older Generation Should Play a Bigger Role Fighting the Debt" by Diane Francis, *Financial Post*, December 8, 1994

When I see a man coming towards me in shorts I cross to the other side of the road.

Anonymous woman writing to the *National Post*

(I know exactly what she means.—**A. Michael Warrington**)

LIFE

An optimist thinks this is the best possible world.
A pessimist fears this is true.

Source Unknown

Memory

Life takes much away from us as through the years we go.
Changes come with changing times—we know it must be so.
But no matter what may come you keep the precious key.
To the private treasure house we call the Memory.

Sent by **Bill Fairs** to *The Guinea Pig*, magazine of the Guinea Pig Club, July, 1995

…this is the Great Theatre of Life. Admission is free but the taxation is mortal. You come when you can and you leave when you must. The show is continuous, good night.

From *The Cunning Man*, **Robertson Davies** (1913–1995)

LILI MARLENE

(German)

Vor de Kaserne
Vor dem großen Tor
Stand eine Laterne
Und steht sie noch davor
So woll'n wir uns da wieder
seh'n
Bei der Laterne wollen wir
steh'n
Wie einst Lili Marleen.

Unsere beide Schatten
Sah'n wie einer aus
Daß wir so lieb uns hatten
Das sah man gleich daraus
Und alle Leute soll'n es seh'n
Wenn wir bei der Laterne
steh'n
Wie einst Lili Marleen.

Schon rief der Posten,
Sie blasen Zapfenstreich
Das kann drei Tage kosten
Kam'rad, ich komm sogleich
Da sagten wir auf Wiedersehen
Wie gerne wollt ich mit dir
geh'n
Mit dir Lili Marleen.

Deine Schritte kennt sie,
Deinen zieren Gang
Alle Abend brennt sie,
Doch mich vergaß sie lang
Und sollte mir ein Leids
gescheh'n

(English Free Translation:
Tommie Connor, 1944)

Underneath the lantern,
By the barrack gate
Darling I remember
The way you used to wait
T'was there that you whispered
tenderly
That you loved me,
You'd always be,
My Lili of the Lamplight,
My own Lili Marlene

Time would come for roll call
Time for us to part,
Darling I'd caress you
And press you to my heart,
And there 'neath that far-off
lantern light
I'd hold you tight,
We'd kiss good night,
My Lili of the Lamplight,
My own Lili Marlene

Orders came for sailing,
Somewhere over there
All confined to barracks
Was more than I could bear
I knew you were waiting in the
street
I heard your feet,
But could not meet,
My Lili of the Lamplight,
My own Lili Marlene

Resting in our billets,

Wer wird bei der Laterne
stehen
Mit dir Lili Marleen?

Just behind the lines
Even tho' we're parted,
Your lips are close to mine

Aus dem stillen Raume,
Aus der Erde Grund

You wait where that lantern
softly gleams
Your sweet face seems

Hebt mich wie im Traume
Dein verliebter Mund
Wenn sich die späten Nebel
drehn
Werd' ich bei der Laterne
steh'n
Wie einst Lili Marleen.

To haunt my dreams
My Lili of the Lamplight,
My own Lili Marlene

—Lili Marlene was a popular war song with a haunting melody. The original German lyrics are from a poem entitled "The Song Of A Young Sentry," composed by a German soldier named Hans Leip in World War I. They were first set to music in 1936 by a composer named Rudolf Zink.

The song was then sung in a Munich restaurant by a Danish cabaret singer named Liselott Wilke, who recorded it in 1940 under her real name, Lale Andersen. Andersen was said to be Swedish, but she was actually a German girl, born in Bremerhaven. The song was broadcast by the German Forces Radio to the Afrika Korps in 1941. It became popular with the British Eighth Army in the North Africa campaign.

LITTLE WORLD

When I was a young man I worked as a reporter and went around all day on a bicycle looking for news stories for the paper.

One day I met a girl, and after that I spent so many hours thinking about how this girl would feel if I became Emperor of Mexico, or maybe died instead, that I had very little time left for anything else. So at night I filled my allotted space with invented stories, which people liked very much because they were much more true to life than true ones. Of course, there is nothing surprising about this, because stories, like people, grow in a certain atmosphere. That's why geography is important.

The stories in this book take place somewhere in the valley of the Po River. I was born near the Po and it is the only respectable river in all Italy. To be respectable, a river must flow through a plain because water was created to stay horizontal and only when it is perfectly horizontal does it preserve its natural dignity. Niagara Falls is an embarrassing phenomenon, like a man who walks on his hands.

Now, the Po crosses the great plains of northern Italy, and in a slice of land between the river and the mountains is a village, a Little World.

People born near the Po River have heads as hard as pig iron, a highly developed sense of humour, and where politics are concerned they can get as excited as a man who has swallowed a mouse. They are very much attached to their slice of land and in spite of floods and fog, the fierce summer heat, and damp winter cold, they admit that, after all, God knew his business when he made the Little World.

This is all the geography that you need in order to understand the village Priest, Don Camillo, and his adversary, Pepponi, the communist mayor, and it is how that Christ watches the goings-on from a big cross in the village church and not infrequently speaks.

And while I am about it, I must say one thing that I always say when I begin to talk about the Little World; if there is a priest anywhere who feels offended by my treatment of Don Camillo, he is welcome to break the biggest candle available over my head. And if there is a Communist who feels offended by Pepponi, he is welcome to break a hammer and sickle on my back. But if there is anyone who is offended by the conversations of Christ, I can't help it; for the one who speaks in this story is not Christ but my Christ—that is, the voice of my conscience.

Don Camillo and the Prodigal Son by **Giovanni Guareschi**

LOVE AND MARRIAGE

Advice to young folk

In a future mate, look for kindness, generosity and affection. Love is admiration, respect and closeness.

Source Unknown

It didn't work out. She married out of her species. She married a jack-ass.

Source Unknown

Marriage

W.C.B. You ask as to what quality should be looked for in choosing a wife.

We would briefly answer: The girl should be religious, industrious, economical, healthy, intelligent, gentle, loving, motherly, a home-builder, a home-lover, suitable, capable, and, above all, a Catholic of the thorough type, able to face adversity as well as prosperity.

From *The Universe*, June 9, 1953

—This item appeared in a Catholic newspaper in England in 1953. At that time I was a final year medical student and I kept the item, indeed, have kept it ever since. In July, 1954, I met Helen at Taplow Hospital, where we were both working. A light went on, and the rest is herstory.—**A. Michael Warrington**

I am a sailor, you're my first mate.
We signed on together, we coupled our fate.
We hauled up our anchor determined not to fail.
For the heart's treasure together we set sail.
We've no maps to guide us we steered our own course.
We rode out the storms when the winds were gale force.
We sat out the doldrums in patience and hope.
Working together we learned how to cope.

Life is an ocean, love is a boat.
In troubled waters it keeps us afloat.
When we started the voyage,
There was just me and you
Now gathered around us, we have our own crew.

Together we're in this relationship
We've built it with care to last the whole trip
Our true destination is not marked on any chart.
We're navigating for the shores of the heart.

Life is an ocean, love is a boat.
In troubled waters it keeps us a float.
When we started the voyage
There was just me and you
Now gathered around us, we have our own crew.

The Voyage, **Johnny Duhan**

LOVE SONGS

<u>My Cup Runneth Over</u>

Sometimes in the morning, when shadows are deep,
I lie here beside you, just watching you sleep.
And sometimes I whisper what I'm thinking of,
My cup runneth over with love.

Sometimes in the evening, when you do not see,
I study the small things, you do constantly,
I memorize moments, that I'm fondest of,
My cup runneth over with love .

In only a moment, we both will be old,
We won't even notice the world turning cold.
And so, in these moments, with sunlight above,
My cup runneth over with love . . .
My cup runneth over with love
With love.

Singer, Ed Ames. Words and music, **Tom Jones** and **Harvey Schmidt**

Wooden Heart

Can't you see
I love you
Please don't break my heart in two
That's not hard to do
'cause I don't have a wooden heart

And if you say goodbye
then I know that I would cry
Maybe I would die
'cause I don't have a wooden heart

There's no strings upon this love of mine
It was always you from the start
Treat me nice
Treat me good
Treat me like you really should
'cause I'm not made of wood
And I don't have a wooden heart

Muss I denn, muss I denn
Zum stadtele hinaus
Stadtele hinaus
Und du, mein schat, bleibst hier?

There's no strings upon this love of mine
It was always you from the start
Sei mir gut
Sei mir gut
Sei mir wie du wirklich sollst
Wie du wirklich sollst
'cause I don't have a wooden heart

German song "*Muss I Denn*" by **Joe Dowell** (English-German version).
Sung by Elvis Presley in *GI Blues* (1960)

Darling, Je Vous Aime Beaucoup

Darling, je vous aime beaucoup
Je ne sais pas what to do
You know you've completely
Stolen my heart

Morning, noon and night-time too
Toujours, wondering what to do
That's the way I've felt
Right from the start

Ah, cherie!
My love for you is très, très fort
Wish my French were good enough
I'd tell you so much more

But I hope that you compris
All the things you mean to me
Darling, je vous aime beaucoup
I love you, yes I do

Wish my French were good enough
I'd tell you so much more

But I hope that you compris
All the things you mean to me
Darling, je vous aime beaucoup

I love you, yes I do
(Darling, je vous aime beaucoup)
I love you, yes I do

Words and music by **Anna Soenko** (1910–2000)

—The song was introduced in the film *Love and Hisses* (1937) by
   Hildegarde, a supper club singer. Hildegarde—simply incomparable!
   How could anyone forget her elegance, her charm? She was the
   most memorable supper club entertainer of the 20th century. She
   knew how to dazzle. Her elegant piano and vocal style, combined
   with flirtatious banter and her champagne smile, made her an icon
   of nightclub sophistication for decades. She was known simply as
   "The Incomparable Hildegarde."

Smoke Gets in Your Eyes

They asked me how I knew,
My true love was true,
I, of course, replied,
Something here inside,
Cannot be denied.

They said some day you'll find
All who love are blind,
When your heart's on fire,
You must realize,
Smoke gets in your eyes.

So I chaffed and I gaily laughed,
To think they could doubt my love,
Yet today, my love has gone away,
I am without my love, without my love,
Now laughing friends deride,
Tears I cannot hide,
Oh, Oh
So I smile and say,
When a lovely flame dies,
Smoke gets in your eyes.

Smoke gets in your eyes,
Smoke gets in your eyes,
Smoke gets in your eyes.

Jeromy Kearn (music), **Otto Harbach** (lyrics)

––––––––––––––––––

MANNERS

Addressing people and, especially patients, by their Christian name
without their permission is presumptuous and inconsiderate.

Professionals, especially doctors, should hold to a certain
formality in approach.

Younger doctors sometimes take the view that the informal
approach makes a patient "relax and enables them to discuss their
problems more freely." With some people it has exactly the opposite
effect and a doctor should first of all ascertain how the patient would
prefer to be addressed.

Adults call children by their first names. Informally addressing
a patient on the first encounter may be seen as identifying the patient
"as in some way inferior to the doctor." A patient's perception of him
or herself as inferior inhibits them from asserting their own right to
participate in treatment decisions.

A. Michael Warrington

––––––––––––––––––

When people take their children to Playspace, there is just one irritating
detail. When you arrive at the wicket to pay your money, the girl pulls
out a big felt marker and an adhesive lapel tag and asks you your name.

"Frum," I say.

"No, your first name."

"What do you need my first name for?"

"I'm going to write it on the tag, so that if any of the children
or any of the staff members need to speak to you, they know what to
call you."

"In that case, write 'Mr. Frum.'"

At which I am given a look as if I had been asked to be called the Duke of Plaza Toro.

In encouraging 5 year olds to address grown-ups by their first names, Playspace is only slightly ahead of the times. Staff at Playspace are engaged in smile-faced acts of belittlement in an assertion of power disguised as bonhomie. Precisely because it is disguised as bonhomie, most people have trouble objecting to first naming, even when it bothers them. First-namers make it clear that they regard anyone who objects to the practice as unspeakably stuffy. Nobody wants to be thought stuffy.

But why not? Stuffiness is having regard for one's dignity. At Playspace, they think it is stuffy of me not to want to be called "David" by my daughter's playmates or by the teenaged girl with a ring through her nose who sells coffee and muffins. To the boorish, self-respect will always seem stuffy. But why should the boors be permitted to make the rules?

David Frum, columnist

Here is a letter from the lady in charge of public relations at one of the largest banks in the United States. "Dear Dave," it starts. I like that even less.

David Frum, columnist

A 70-year-old man who buys a hamburger at Lick's will be first-named by the teenager behind the counter. Habitual first-namers claim they are motivated by nothing worse than uncontrollably exuberant friendliness. I don't believe it. If I asked the order-takers at Lick's to lend me $50 their friendliness would vanish in a whoosh.

David Frum, columnist

Grandma Knows Best

My mother believed in the most old fashioned of all principles of etiquette: the written thank you note.

When my niece, Maura, had her first child, my mother sent a card and a cheque as a gift to her new great-granddaughter. The cheque cleared the bank so Mum knew someone had received it. But she heard nothing from Maura.

Several months later, I told my mother about Maura's impatient response when I asked her if she had sent a thank you card to her grandma: "Aunt Maggie, I sent Grandma a 'cosmic' thank you."

Mum paused.

"Tell Maura that next time, I'll send her a cosmic cheque."

Maggie Bedrosiam, *Chocolate For a Woman's Soul*

Knowledge speaks but wisdom listens.

Jimi Hendrix (1942–1970)

Politeness is to do and say
The kindest thing in the kindest way.

Source Unknown

If you pick up a starving dog and make him prosperous, he will not bite you.
This is the principal difference between a dog and a man.

Mark Twain

MEDICINE

Quotations from Sir William Osler

A physician who treats himself has a fool for a patient.

The greatest gift that nature or grace can bestow on a man is the *aequus animus*, the even-balanced soul; but unfortunately nature rather than grace, disposition rather than education, determines its existence. I cannot agree.... that it is not to be acquired. On the contrary, I maintain that much may be done to cultivate a cheerful heart.

The practice of medicine is an art, not a trade; a calling, not a business; a calling in which your heart will be exercised equally with your head.

To study the phenomena of disease without books is to sail an uncharted sea, while to study books without patients is not to go to sea at all.

In some of us the ceaseless panorama of suffering tends to dull that fine edge of sympathy with which we started .... Against this benumbing influence, we physicians and nurses, the immediate agents of the Trust, have but one enduring corrective—the practice towards patients of the Golden Rule of Humanity as announced by Confucius (6th Century B.C. Chinese Philosopher): "What you do not like when done to yourself, do not do to others."

The art of the practice of medicine is to be learned only by experience; it is not an inheritance; it cannot be revealed. Learn to see, learn to hear, learn to feel, learn to smell and know that by practice alone can you become expert.

Once gain the confidence of a patient and inspire him with hope, and the battle is half won.

There are only two sorts of doctors; those who practice with their brains, and those who practice with their tongues.

It is so much easier to do a penny-in-the-slot sort of practice in which each symptom is at once met by its appropriate drug than to make a careful examination and really to study the case systematically.

The cultivated general practitioner. May this be the destiny of a large majority of you! You cannot reach any better position in a community; the family doctor is "the man behind the gun," who does our effective work. That his life is hard and exacting; that he is underpaid and overworked; that he has but little time for study and less for recreation—these are the blows that may give finer temper to his steel, and bring out the noble elements in his character.

In no relationship is the physician more often derelict than in his duty to himself.

Remember, however, that every patient upon whom you wait will examine you critically and form an estimate of you by the way in which you conduct yourself at the bedside. Skill and nicety and manipulation, whether in the simple act of feeling the pulse, or in the performance of any minor operation will do more towards establishing confidence in you, than a string of diplomas, or the reputation of extensive hospital experience.

The conditions of modern life favour arteriosclerosis as a man is apt to work his body machine at high pressure and often takes less care of it than of his motor.

There are two essential factors in arteriosclerosis—the quality of the tubing and the way it is treated. The marvel is that any set of pipes could be constructed to stand the continuous strain to which for years the human blood vessels are subjected. The contract calls for from 60 to 80 years of usage. Some hold out well and even after 90 years are still fairly good, but the personal equation has always to be considered.

More commonly the arteriosclerosis results from the bad use of good vessels.

Nothing is more certain than that the pace of modern life kills many prematurely through the complications of arteriosclerosis. The keen, sharp business or professional man, year in, year out, giving his energies no rest, leading a life of high pressure, though a teetotaller and tempered in his diet and a non-smoker, may have so driven his machine that at 50 it is only fit to be scrapped.

———————————

Lessen the intake. We all eat too much and in no age were the saying more true that "the platter kills more that the sword." People habitually eat too much and it is probably true that a greater number of maladies arise from excess in eating than from excess in drinking.

———————————

We are all dietetic sinners; only a small percent of what we eat nourishes us, the balance goes to waste and loss of energy.

———————————

Patients should have rest, food, fresh air and exercise—the quadrangle of health.

———————————

Man has an inborn craving for medicine... The desire to take medicine is one feature which distinguishes man, the animal, from his fellow creatures.

———————————

While on the one hand I would encourage you with the firmest faith in a few drugs ("the friends you have and their adoption tried"). On the other hand, I would urge you to cultivate a keenly sceptical attitude towards the pharmacopoeia, remembering the shrewd remark of Benjamin Franklin that, "He is the best doctor who knows the worthlessness of the most medicines."

———————————

The young physician starts life with 20 drugs for each disease, and the old physician ends life with one drug for 20 diseases.

———————————

The battle against polypharmacy, or the use of a large number of drugs (the action of which we know little, yet we put them into bodies, the action of which we know less), has not been fought to a finish.

In therapeutics we do not so much need new remedies as a fuller knowledge of when and how to use the old ones.

The hardest conviction to get into the mind of a beginner is that the education upon which he is engaged is not a college course, not a medical course, but a life course, for which the work of a few years under teachers is but a preparation.

At the outset it is necessary for you to bear in mind that your professional education (on graduation) is by no means complete; you have, as it were, only laid the foundation and...while it is to be hoped that a good and promising foundation has been laid under the guidance and instruction of others, it rests with yourselves what the superstructure shall be.

Medicine is a most difficult art to acquire. All a college can do is to teach the student principles, based on facts in science, and give him good methods of work. These simply start him in the right direction, they do not make a good practitioner—that is his own affair. To master the art requires sustained effort, like the bird's flight which depends on the incessant action of the wings, but this sustained effort is so hard that many give up the struggle in despair.

The training of the medical school gives a man his direction, points him the way, and furnishes him with a chart, fairly incomplete, for the voyage, but nothing more.

There is no higher mission in life than nursing.

Caring is an old tradition;
Nursing as a profession is new.

Gentleness is the nurse's birthright. It is expressed by words, by hand, or in motion.
Sir William Osler (1849–1919)

—One of the greatest physicians who ever lived.

_____

From inability to let well alone;
From too much zeal for the new and contempt for what is old;
From putting knowledge before wisdom, science before art and cleverness before common sense;
From treating patients as cases and from making the cure of the disease more grievous than the endurance of the same, Good Lord, deliver us.

Sir Robert Hutchison (1871–1960), English physician

_____

Dispatch from the Medical Front

To our multi-national group of eight this seemed like a windfall. Our grand foray to the Great Wall of China was to be interrupted by an unscheduled stop at the world-renowned Imperial Academy of Natural Chinese Medicine.

We were greeted warmly by a pair of attractive young women in freshly starched lab coats, ushered into a classroom, served a hot beverage made from "health giving" plants and treated to a lecture lauding Chinese Traditional and Natural Medicine. We learned about Ying and Yang, the ethicacy of acupuncture and the incomparable excellence of hospital staff.

Then, as a special gift, we Western visitors received a free, personal examination from two of the Academy's most renowned professors: A and B.

They arrived, dapper in suits and lab coats. The two attractive women encouraged us to clap. Disappointed by our lack of vigour, A instructed us to clap harder. He motioned me forward. The translator ordered me to extend my hand, palm up, on a soiled pink satin cushion. My pulse was taken, my tongue examined. A asked my age and gravely inquired about my current medications. A look of disapproval crossed his face when I told him that I did not take anything.

"Very serious," he intoned. "You have overheated liver, sluggish circulation and thick blood."

I protested that I felt very well.

"Very serious," the interpreter repeated. "No energy, fatigue, dry mouth and sometimes forget things."

A sadly shook his head.

Again I protested: The weather was hot, my energy excellent, my memory good.

"Sometimes," he implored, "the most serious of medical conditions seem like that until it is too late. You need urgent treatment."

I explained that our bus was moving on. He urged me to "Look after your health before it is too late...hundreds of my patients come to my hospital from North America before it is too late."

I was clearly not a good patient.

Other patients were summoned forward. A Mexican doctor was diagnosed with "serious womb and period problems." Also of a non-compliant bent, she was swiftly discharged, as was another Canadian physician suffering "sluggish circulation, hypertension, thick blood and developing diabetes." He protested that he felt well and recent lab work was normal. But a muscular, 35-year-old dental technician grew more responsive. Advised that he was "seriously ill, hypertension, sluggish circulation and on the verge of getting diabetes," he forked over $300 US for a football sized bag of dried herbs. He was instructed to return "without fail" in three months. He looked worried!

Donna Stewart, M.D., Toronto, Ontario in the *Canadian Medical Association Journal*, January 29, 2008

Thought For the Day

There is an independent judiciary. There should be an independent medical profession.

A. Michael Warrington

MISTAKEN IDENTITY

A medical student was doing a rotation in psychiatry in Montreal. As part of their training, medical students are required to take histories from patients and make an evaluation in order to arrive at a diagnosis. The following is an actual account of an interview with a patient.

Student: "What can I help you with?"
Patient: "I'm having a problem at work."
Student: "What sort of problem?"
Patient: "The dishwasher keeps talking to me."
The student made a note—Auditory hallucinations—and, in the cautious tone of voice that you use when talking to someone who appears to be a little crazy: "What does the dishwasher talk about?"
Patient: "Things like: I don't know how to do my job and where did I learn to cook?"
The student made another note—Paranoid delusions of persecution.
Patient: "… he says I should be fired."
Student: "Who says you should be fired?"
Patient: "Henri."
Student: "Who's Henri?"
Patient: "The dishwasher!"
The penny drops—the student then had to make a rapid mental adjustment without letting on that he thought all along that the patient was talking about a kitchen appliance.

—True story. For confidentiality reasons, cannot identify medical
    student or patient by name—**A. Michael Warrington**

Talking Dishwasher

MONEY

Money doesn't bring happiness, but at least you can be miserable in comfort.

A. Michael Warrington

They say money talks, but the only thing it ever said to me was good-bye.

Source Unknown

MORALITY

For these are not things of yesterday or tomorrow but are for all time.

Antigone by **Sophocles**

MUSINGS

A day without sunshine is like night.

Source Unknown

It is frustrating when you know all the answers but nobody bothers to ask you the questions.

Source Unknown

Nor for my peace will I go far,
As wanderers do, that still do roam;
But make my strengths, such as they are, here in my bosom, and at
home.

Ben Jonson (1572–1637), dramatist and poet

Brain cells come and go but fat cells live forever.

Source Unknown

Dieting is just mind over fatter.

Source Unknown

Menu Choices

A spectacled, rumple-haired elderly gentleman sat down at the
restaurant table beside me. He had the gentle, unworldly appearance of
a Professor of Metaphysics or maybe an old chess champion.

With a big sigh, he thoughtfully leaned my way and studied
most shrewdly what was on my plate. Then he picked up the menu
and, holding it close to his eyes, he read it from top to bottom, item by
item, from the tomato juice right down to tea, coffee or milk.

By the time the waitress arrived to take his order, he appeared
to have made up his mind.

"I will have two eggs any style," he said firmly.

The waitress was a little shaken.

"Which style?" she asked.

The old gentleman picked the menu up, scanned it intently, and
then pointing with his fingertip, he held it up for the waitress to see.

"This," he said patiently. "'Two eggs any style', it says."

"Yes," said the waitress, "but that only means we can serve
them any style."

"I'm sure you can," said the old gentleman. "That's the way I
would like them, please."

"But," explained the girl, bending down, "you have to choose

Menu Choices

which style."

"Oh, dear," sighed he.

So he ordered liver and bacon.

Gregory Clark

Humankind makes a poorer performance of Government than almost any other human activity.

Barbara Tuchman

A teacher affects eternity; he can never tell where his influence stops.

Henry B. Adams

What I Would Like to Hear at My Funeral

After dying in a car crash, three friends go to heaven for orientation and they are all asked the same question: "When you are in your coffin and friends and family are mourning you, what would you like them to say about you?"

The first person immediately responds, "I would like to hear them say that I was one of the greatest doctors of my time and a great family man."

The second person says, "I would like to hear that I was a wonderful husband and school teacher who made a huge difference in our children of tomorrow."

The last man thinks a minute and replies, "I would like to hear them say...'LOOK!!! HE'S MOVING!!!'"

Source Unknown

I told you I was sick.

Comical epitaph first coined by **W.C. Fields**.

On the factional nationalism of the Edwardian Age: "'My country, right or wrong', is a thing that no patriot would think of saying except in a desperate case. It is like saying, 'my mother, drunk or sober.'"

On being controversial: "I believe in getting into hot water, it keeps you clean."

A citizen can hardly distinguish between a tax and a fine except that the fine is generally much lighter.

Journalism largely consists of saying "Lord Jones is dead" to people who never knew that Lord Jones was alive.

G. K. Chesterton (1874–1936), English writer

He is neither first-rate, nor second-rate, nor tenth-rate. He is just his horrible, unique self.

George Bernard Shaw, writing about someone that he did not particularly like.

Committee—A group of men who individually can do nothing but as a group decide that nothing can be done.

Source Unknown

NEWS ITEMS

Pupil, 84, Faces Expulsion from Elementary School

The world's oldest grade school student, an octogenarian great-grandfather, is facing expulsion from an elementary school in Kenya after parents complained that he was a disruptive influence in the classroom.

Penniless and illiterate, Kimani Maruge, who is aged 84, turned up last year at a primary school in western Kenya demanding to be enrolled in the first grade.

Mr. Maruge said he had not been able to attend school as a boy because he had to look after the cattle, and could only now attend school after the government abolished elementary school fees in 2003.

Cutting off the bottoms of his only pants, and splurging on a pair of grey, knee length socks to meet the dress code, Mr. Maruge lined up with more that 100 six year olds to be registered.

"I was impressed by his desire to learn and gave him a place," said the school principal.

He was popular with the other students and the teachers and he was made a prefect. But when he began his second year, some parents protested.

Mr. Maruge was a "smart Alec," prone to histrionics, one parent said.

"Our children don't concentrate", the parent said. "They are too busy wondering what he is going to do next."

News item in *The Daily Telegraph*, January, 2005

Amanda Montei, 24, of Birkenhead, Merseyside in England admitted ripping off her ex-lover's testicle after he refused to have sex with her. She yanked off the left testicle of Geoffrey Jones, 37, which was later handed to him by a friend. Montei will be sentenced next month.

Guardian Weekly, January 14–20, 2005

NEVER ARGUE WITH A WOMAN

One morning a husband returns after several hours of fishing and decides to take a nap.

Although not familiar with the lake, his wife decides to take the boat out. She motors out a short distance, anchors and reads her book.

Along comes a game warden in his boat. He pulls up alongside the woman and says, "Good morning, ma'am. What are you doing?"

"Reading a book," she replies, thinking, isn't that obvious?

"You're in a restricted fishing area," he informs her.

"I'm sorry, officer, but I'm not fishing. I am reading."

"Yes, but you have all the equipment. For all I know you could start at any moment. I'll have to take you in and write this up."

"If you do that, I'll have to charge you with sexual assault," says the woman.

"But I haven't even touched you," says the game warden.

"That's true, but you have all the equipment. For all I know you could start at any moment."

"Have a nice day, ma'am." And he leaves.

—Moral: Never argue with a woman who is reading; it is a sign that she can also think.

NEWSPAPER COLUMNS

I've never been able to handle that word, genitalia. It sounds to me like a chilled Italian dessert.

I like the crows that run my beach. The way they stomp around importantly in their gloomy black feather suits, they remind me of members of the Senate, trying to give the solemn impression of doing work.

Denny Boyd, columnist for *The Vancouver Sun*, on the occasion of his retirement, June, 1995

Another bastion fell last Wednesday when a woman refereed an important soccer match for the first time. Carolina Domenech officiated in the game between Real Madrid and Atletico Madrid, and not surprisingly, nothing untoward happened. No one abused her, flare ups between the players were rare and she refereed in a fluent and imaginative way. So why was the world's most popular sport so slow to take the sort of step which can only improve it and diminish violence on the field? After all, male players are unlikely to mob a woman referee over a decision they don't like. But they can easily accost male referees, in part because soccer protests are usually exercises in violence. Equally, males are programmed socially and probably genetically not to behave like that towards women, not least because women don't go to war. Or, rather didn't, until recently.

Any bus service will confirm that women conductors, or conductresses as they used to charmingly be known, have less trouble with drunks and yobs than their male colleagues. Conductresses can exercise command without threat to the maleness of their passengers. Similarly, since women referees present no challenge to the powerful macho instincts of professional footballers, the latter are much less likely to confront them, regardless of their refereeing decisions. This does not mean women lack authority. Indeed it comes naturally to many women.

Women referees will probably not just mean better behaved footballers, but better behaved crowds. Men in crowds don't like shouting vituperation at women. Even the most virulently anti-Thatcher mobs barely manage better than "Maggie, Maggie, Maggie" which is about as earth shattering as Christopher Robin giving someone a good ticking off.

But having women soccer referees does not mean having women soccer players playing alongside men. The male warrior, Ethos, is at the heart of aggressive, competitive soccer. What man is going to go into a hard, bone-breaking tackle with a woman? The violence, symbolic and real, are male things which tend to exclude women, though they do not prevent women having a go in their own games of soccer.

The success of Carolina Domenech should teach us that women and men are best served by playing to their own complementary strengths, not doing the reverse and ignoring them.

Kevin Myers, *Sunday Telegraph*, January 6, 2002

Boxing

It is the "why" question that remains unanswered, and for any boxer, that's everything. This sport instantly weeds out the fakers and the poseurs, the guy's doing it only for the paycheque or the glory.

There is no going through the motions. Any lack of commitment becomes obvious sooner or later, not just for the audience, but to the guy standing in the opposite corner. And that's why the greatest fighters are a special breed—they are willing to do what most of most of us are not.

Stephen Brunt, "The Game," *Globe and Mail*, May 5, 2007

NOSTALGIA

That is the land of lost content,
I see it shining plain,
The happy highway's where I went,
And cannot come again.

A. E. Housman (1859–1936), poet

I remember my youth and the feeling that will never come back anymore—the feeling that I could last forever—the glow in the heart that with every year grows dim, grows cold, grows small and expires—and expires, too soon, too soon—before life itself.

Joseph Conrad in *Youth*

We all have to learn to say good bye to the past and be grown up about it. But for me, it is not just my family house that is gone; it is a whole way of life, a recollection of the way things used to be in the sunny days when I was young.

Mary Kenny, writing in the *Sunday Telegraph*

Jenny kissed me when we met,
Jumping from the chair she sat in;
Time you thief, who loved to get
Sweets into your list, put that in:
Say I'm weary, say I'm sad,
Say that health and wealth have missed me,

Say I'm growing old, but add
Jenny kissed me.

Leigh Hunt (1784–1859), English poet and essayist

OLYMPIC GAMES

<u>On London Being a Projected Host</u>

We now know that the Greek Games (the hundreds of medallists from which almost no one now remembers) cost 11.6 billion Euros—twice the original budget. This was more than 5% of Greece's Gross Domestic Product, and alone pushed the Greek budget deficit to 5.3%, nearing double the ceiling allowed by E.U. rules.

For this is the certain truth: the Olympic Games are economically and socially ruinous for their hosts. Only a pride-fuelled dementia would induce any city to wish to host them. Sydney, whose games in 2000 are called "successful" is still paying $32 million dollars a year merely to maintain the now chronically under-utilized stadiums. China is budgeting $23 billion for the Games in 2008—which probably won't cover security costs.

But equally relevant is: Why? What is the true purpose of the Olympic games? Who remembers who won the women's smooth-bore tobogganing medal, apart from her mother? Who knows now who got the gold in the 200 metres dog-shooting? Who recalls who triumphed in the men's downhill knitting at Athens, or the ladies Excuse Me, or the light heavyweight Gay Gordon's?

It's not as if the ephemerality of the results is unimportant beside the goodwill generated by the Olympian spirit. For—even putting the terrorist threat aside—that is dead, poisoned by a rancid nationalism and a culture of cheating, especially in athletics, swimming and weight lifting. If you unquestioningly accept world records set in any race under 800 metres, in a strength contest of any kind, or anything in the pool over the past 20 years, then you also probably believe Elvis is running a guest house in Leighton Buzzard.

All this—the drugs, the terrorist threat, the economy-wreaking costs, the witless chauvinism, the cynicism—is part of the real Olympian spirit of today. It is beyond all parody.

Life in London—by all accounts—is already unbearable. Do Londoners really want the horrors of the Games visited on them? Do they want to be paying for the upkeep of unused velodromes and empty equestrian rinks and deserted pogo-stick courts into the indefinite future, little baby-Millennium-domes at which visitors will split their sides laughing?

Londoners who didn't have the wit to hurl custard pies…at the I.O.C. delegation should now be on their knees praying that either Madrid, Paris, New York or Moscow gets the Games. The Olympics is the last thing London needs.

Kevin Myers writing in the *Sunday Telegraph*, February 20, 2005

PASSING THE TEST

To everyone a gift is given and a problem set.
There is a mission to fulfil, a challenge to be met.
A special work to carry out that no one else can do.
A task to be accomplished and to this we must be true.

Patience Strong (1907–1990), English poet

PERSISTENCE

Nothing in the world can take the place of persistence.
Talent will not; nothing is more common than unsuccessful men with
    talent.
Genius will not; unrewarded genius is almost a proverb.
Education will not; the world is full of educated derelicts.
Persistence and determination alone are omnipotent.

The slogan "Press On" has solved and always will solve the problems of the human race.

Source Unknown

POETRY

He Wishes for the Cloths of Heaven

Had I the heavens' embroidered cloths,
Enwrought with golden and silver light,
The blue and the dim and the dark cloths
Of night and light and the half-light,
I would spread the cloths under your feet:
But I, being poor, have only my dreams;
I have spread my dreams under your feet;
Tread softly because you tread on my dreams.

W.B. Yeats (1865–1939), Irish poet

And I shall have some peace there, for peace comes dropping slow.
Dropping from the veils of the morning to where the cricket sings;
There midnight's all a-glimmer and noon a purple glow,
And evening full of the linnet's wings.

From *The Lake Isle of Innisfree*, **W.B. Yates** (1865–1939), Irish poet

---

Lines written beneath an Elm in the Churchyard of Harrow

Spot of my youth! whose hoary branches sigh,
Swept by the breeze that fans thy cloudless sky:
Where now alone I muse, who oft have trod,
With those I loved, thy soft and verdant sod;
With those who, scattered far, perchance deplore,
Like me, the happy scenes they knew before:

Oh! as I trace again thy winding hill,
Mine eyes admire, my heart adores thee still,
Thou drooping Elm! beneath whose boughs I lay,
And frequent mused the twilight hours away:
Where, as they once were wont, my limbs recline,
But ah! without the thoughts which then were mine.
How do thy branches, moaning to the blast,
Invite the bosom to recall the past,
And seem to whisper, as they gently swell,
"Take, while thou canst, a lingering, last farewell!"

When Fate shall chill, at length, this fever'd breast,
And calm its cares and passions into rest,
Oft have I thought, 'twould soothe my dying hour,--
If aught may soothe, when Life resigns her power,--
To know some humbler grave, some narrow cell,
Would hide my bosom where it lov'd to dwell;
With this fond dream, methinks 'twere sweet to die--
And here it linger'd, here my heart might lie;
Here might I sleep where all my hopes arose,
Scene of my youth, and couch of my repose;
For ever stretch'd beneath this mantling shade,
Press'd by the turf where once my childhood play'd;
Wrapt by the soil that veils the spot I lov'd,
Mix'd with the earth o'er which my footsteps mov'd;
Blest by the tongues that charm'd my youthful ear,
Mourn'd by the few my soul acknowledged here;
Deplor'd by those in early days allied,
And unremember'd by the world beside.

Lord Byron (1728–1824), English poet

An English Cottage

I passed beneath the lintel of an ancient gnarled oak door,
As others over centuries had passed that way before.
I trod across the stone-flagged floor—where sunlit shadows fell
Through latticed windows dimmed with age, where misted memories
   dwell.

An inglenook with open hearth, and twisted chimney tall;
A spinning wheel from bygone days, and a settle in the hall.
And in a cupboard quaint and old—a secret stair I found,
That led to rooms beneath the eaves, with knotted black beams
    crowned.

The gentle breeze of England swept throughout these haunted rooms,
The scent of herbs and lavender, are fragrant rose's bloom.
And I thought from out the past I heard a rustle on the stair,
As though someone was pleased that I had stopped to visit there.

Beryl Shepard Leece

No man is an island, entire of itself;
Every man is a piece of the continent, a part of the main;
If a clod be washed away by the sea, Europe is the less....
Any man's death diminishes me, because I am involved in mankind;
And therefore, never send to know for whom the bell tolls;
It tolls for thee.

John Donne (1573–1631), English poet

The Listeners

"Is there anybody there?" said the Traveller,
Knocking on the moonlit door;
And his horse in the silence champed the grasses,
Of the forest's ferny floor:
And a bird flew up out of the turret,
Above the Traveller's head;
And he smote upon the door a second time;
"Is there anybody there?" he said.
But no one descended to the Traveller;
No head from the leaf-fringed sill
Leaned over and looked into his grey eyes,
Where he stood perplexed and still.

But only a host of phantom listeners
That dwelt in the lone house then
Stood listening in the quiet of the moonlight
To that voice from the world of men:

Stood thronging the faint moonbeams on the dark stair,
That goes down to the empty hall,
Hearkening in an air stirred and shaken
By the lonely Traveller's call.
And he felt in his heart their strangeness,
Their stillness answering his cry,
While his horse moved, cropping the dark turf,
'Neath the starred and leafy sky;
For he suddenly smote on the door, even
Louder, and lifted his head:
"Tell them I came, and no one answered,
That I kept my word," he said.
Never the least stir made the listeners,
Though every word he spake
Fell echoing through the shadowiness of the still house
From the one man left awake:
Ay, they heard his foot upon the stirrup,
And the sound of iron on stone,
And how the silence surged softly backward,
When the plunging hoofs were gone.

Walter de la Mare (1873–1958) English novelist and poet

Sea Fever

I must down to the sea again, to the lonely sea and the sky,
And all I ask is a tall ship and a star to steer her by,
And the wheel's kick and the wind's song and the white sail's shaking,
And a grey mist on the sea face, and a grey dawn breaking.

I must down to the sea again, for the call of the running tide
Is a wild call and a clear call that may not be denied;
And all I ask is a windy day with the white clouds flying,
And the flung spray and the blown spume, and the sea-gulls crying.

I must down to the sea again, to the vagrant gypsy life,
To the gull's way and the whale's way where the wind's like a whetted
    knife;
And all I ask is a merry yarn from a laughing fellow-rover
And quiet sleep and a sweet dream when the long trick's over.

John Masefield (1878–1967), English poet and novelist

—Born at Ledbury, Herefordshire, educated at King's School,
    Warwick and on the training ship *H.M.S. Conway*. He was
    apprenticed aboard a windjammer, but when he was in New York
    he left the sea and lived for several years in the United States before
    returning to England. He was only 22 years old when he wrote *Sea
    Fever*. He became Poet Laureate in 1930.

The Wanderers

Oh then I'll wander back again
        and seek the place I knew
When all the world was young and fair
        and all the tales were true

Rudolph Chambers Lehmann (1856–1929), English poet

If

If you can keep your head when all about you
Are losing theirs and blaming it on you,
If you can trust yourself when all men doubt you,
But make allowance for their doubting too:

If you can wait and not be tired by waiting,
Or being lied about, don't deal in lies,
Or being hated, don't give way to hating,
And yet don't look too good, nor talk too wise;

If you can dream—and not make dreams your master;
If you can think—and not make thoughts your aim;

If you can meet with Triumph and Disaster
And treat those two impostors just the same;
If you can bear to hear the truth you have spoken twisted by knaves to
   make a trap for fools,
Or watch the things you gave your life to, broken,
And stoop and build 'em up with worn-out tools:

If you can make one heap of all of your winnings
And risk it on one turn of pitch-and-toss
And lose, and start again at your beginnings
And never breath a word about your loss;
If you can force your heart and nerve and sinew
To serve your term long after they are gone,
And so hold on when there is nothing in you
Except the Will that says to them: "Hold on!"

If you can talk with crowds and keep your virtue,
Or walk with Kings—nor lose the common touch
If neither foes nor loving friends can hurt you
If all men count with you, but none too much;
If you can fill the unforgiving minute
With sixty seconds worth of distance run
Yours is the Earth and everything that's in it,
And—which is more—you will be a Man, my son!

Rudyard Kipling (1986–1936). English author and poet

—Among Kipling's many works: *The Jungle Book, Just So Stories, The Man
   Who Would be King* and the poem *Gunga Din* ("You're a Better Man
   Than I Am Gunga Din"). In 1915 his only son, John, was killed in
   the Battle of Loos. Kipling joined the Imperial War Graves
   Commission (now the Commonwealth War Graves Commission)—
   the group responsible for the garden-like British war graves that
   exist to this day along the former Western Front and other locations
   around the world where Commonwealth troops lie buried. His most
   significant contribution to this project was his selection of the
   Biblical phrase "Their Name Liveth For Evermore" found on
   cenotaphs and Stones of Remembrance.

There once was a doctor named Warrington,
Whose bedside manner should have been in quarantine,
How he ever got to eight,
When he'd work here so late,
A very busy doc was our Warrington!

Marg Fenney, RN, Emergency Room, Lion's Gate Hospital, 1971

POLITICS

Politicians and diapers have one thing in common.
They should both be changed regularly and for the same reason.

Source Unknown

I was politically-minded to some extent but never able to put politics
first, always repelled, not attracted by the political life. There are
various reasons why a youngster may find a political atmosphere and
political activities irresistible: He may be a blazing fanatic; he may be
hungry for power on any level; he may be ambitious without
possessing any particular talent; he may delight in intrigue, happiest
when arranging with Smith and Brown to keep out Robinson; and he
may combine all of these so that in the end, at our expense, he gets the
jackpot.

From *Margin Released* by **J.B. Priestley** (1894–1984), English journalist
and playwright

A Liberal is a man too broad-minded to take his own side in a quarrel.

Robert Frost

THE POTATO IN HISTORY

Why was President Kennedy an American? Because of the potato.

The potato, Solanum tuberonun, is a plant native to high altitudes, with thin soil and short days, low temperatures at night and a dry atmosphere.

In Western Europe it flourishes in moist, cool atmospheres, with relatively long days and warm nights, and enjoys a deep, friable soil. In poor soil, potatoes are much more suitable than grain crops. Few tools are needed: In an emergency, a crop can be grown and harvested with one's bare hands. Nor do potatoes need threshing, grinding or baking; a pot and a peat fire are enough.

The poorer people who survived most successfully in Ireland were probably those who, by observation and trial and error, had gathered stocks of potatoes which were best adapted to the conditions found in the poorer areas of the island. The Irish people needed every adaptation of which they—and the potato—were capable.

The "lazy bed" can be prepared on any kind of ground, almost anywhere. The land need not be flat, and stones do not inhibit potato growing as they do in normal fields. A strip of land, from two feet wide in very wet soil to as much as six to seven feet wide in dry soils, is spread with whatever manure may be available: seaweed, the rotted turf of an old house, or dry peat. A ditch is dug on either side and the earth from it is thrown up on top of the manure. The bed is now self draining and the potatoes have been "riched up" before they have been planted.

A strip between 500 and 800 yards long would provide more than enough potatoes for one family. Supplemented with milk, pork, bacon, cheese, they would provide a balanced diet for a typical family.

The lazy bed had many advantages. Half an acre could provide in a normal year for a normal family. It was immune to frost, well drained and well manured. After the potatoes had stopped growing, the lazy bed came into its own which needed only to be dug as required and then go straight into the pot.

If the worst came to the worst and the man, having spent the Summer in the hills, was unable to return home at harvest time, the lazy bed would be full of potatoes by the following Spring.

The lazy bed was so-called because not all the ground had to be tilled: About half the area had inverted sods placed upon the unbroken soil.

The English, through ignorance or malice, thought the lazy bed an idler's way to grow potatoes; it became a drawing room joke about the Irish.

If the potatoes produced in a lazy bed were a family's only source of food, the only cash a man would need would be to pay his rent to the landlord (often absentee landlords in England).

In 1660, the population in Ireland was probably about half a million. By 1688 the population had more than doubled to 1.25 million.

As the Irishman had no regular work, without the potato and the do-it-yourself cabin, the population could never have survived, let alone increased.

Between 1760 and 1840, the population in Ireland increased from 1.5 million to 9 million. This had everything to do with the potato. Without the potato, all the land in Ireland could at most have enabled only 5 million to be fed with bread. This was at a period of worldwide shortages of bread grains at a price which the Irish could afford. Grain in Europe as a whole doubled in price between 1760 and 1840.

The position of Ireland in 1854 to 1846, the first winter of the Great Famine, was characteristic—unless such an approaching disaster is recognized while the indigenous population is strong enough to solicit outside help to prevent it, famine is inevitable. But at this stage of the Irish Famine, there was insufficient public sympathy to attract assistance and by the time sympathy had been aroused, it was too late for anyone to prevent the catastrophe.

Half the population depended on the potato for more than three quarters of their energy requirements.

The real killer of potatoes was blight. It reappeared continuously at intervals until micro-biologists and agricultural experts found the cure. But this was not until the 1920s.

For four or five years after the first attack of the blight in the 1940s, Ireland was wracked by the agony of famine, disease and depopulation. Emigration continued for a long time. Up to a million men, women and children are estimated to have died from starvation or cholera or one of the other diseases that follow in famine's wake.

Up to 1.5 million Irish left the country as a direct result of the Famine, setting a pattern of continuing emigration for the rest of the century.

By 1914, some 5.5 million people would have left Ireland. The history of both Britain and the United States was fundamentally altered by this situation.

This was the worst recorded famine to take place in Ireland because, though there had been no fewer than 27 famines in the previous 100 years and five in the preceding ten years, and their frequency was accelerating, these other famines were all local. The disaster of 1845 was not only the first recorded island-wide potato failure, but from some point in the Autumn of that year, for the first time in history, there were no potatoes for sale anywhere in Europe—for two years virtually none were fit for market.

People have since wondered at the contemporary inability to see what was needed and what could have been provided. How much of the Irish tragedy was the result of "invincible ignorance."

In 1797, England had the best infrastructure in the world. Ireland had one of the worst infrastructures in Europe. Hunger was not only a question of growing food, but more importantly a question of harvest, distribution and exchange. The Irish peasant grew his own food and was outside the network of distribution and cash exchange. What then would happen if the potato crop failed? Between 1797 and 1995, there were 20 failures of the potato crop. All of them involving some deaths from starvation, disease or debility; all of these years would be classed today as famines. In twenty years out of forty-eight years there were famines in Ireland, but only three in England. In America, the Irish influence has become so much a part of political life as to be taken for granted, but before the 1840s the whites in the new nation were overwhelmingly Protestant, Nordic or Anglo Saxon, from England, Scotland, Wales, Ulster, Holland, Germany and Scandinavia, with a few pockets of French, German, Spanish and Swiss Catholics. A proportion of these would have been Irish and Catholic.

The flood of Catholic Irish began in the 1840s. In the fifteen years between the famine and the American Civil War, Irish incomers reached a total of more than 100,000 a year. They made a difference to the new nation, not only in terms of numbers (about 5 percent of the population of those States which they entered) but also as a proportion of the favoured cities (about 30 percent). Boston and New York were often the first places the steerage passenger would see and there he often stayed.

The immigrants were often destitute, unskilled labourers, without homes to go to and with few friends and relations to help them. They had, perhaps, been the survivors of several years of starvation, certainly several years of protein shortage and exposure to typhus or pneumonia. They huddled together in Irish Catholic ghettos. The Priest was their friend on Sunday and the local politician their amiable exploiter during the week. This group of potential voters could be massaged into blocks of great political power, which still influence the cities that first sheltered them. Out of the sub-culture which they formed came, in the next two generations, rich and powerful politicians and propertymen, and their Celtic qualities were in no way diminished by this significant urbanization of the Irish Catholic character.

In America, the Irish peasant, who had grimly endured the whole previous generation, became a legitimate citizen whose vote was canvassed, whose needs were met and whose importance was freely acknowledged.

It took time to overcome the appalling conditions which had driven the immigrants to leave the bogs and the mountains of Ireland, but a new and amazing vigour and enterprise was evident in every industry and service into which they entered: railroads, textiles, mining, contracting, building, civil engineering and the police, as well as politics.

The art of talking a hind leg off a donkey was given full rein and wordy rhetoric, so characteristic of the public man in the later 19th Century, became more fashionable than anywhere else in those cities with a large Irish Catholic element. The native Irish enjoyed it all, whether the rhetoric was their own or that of some politician of another ethnic group soliciting their support. The Irish heightened political volatility and strengthened the American belief that any action is justified by success.

Of all the immigrants into the United States at a time when a high proportion of Americans were of Anglo-Saxon Protestant origin, the Irish were the only politically organized, ethnically integrated group motivated by dislike for England.

There was every reason for these unhappy refugees to dislike England.

Long before Cromwell's time during the 16th and 17th Centuries most of the land in Ireland was confiscated from Irish Catholic land owners and given to British settlers. The seized land was given to English nobles and soldiers, some of whom rented it out to Irishmen while they themselves remained residents of England. The existence of absentee landlords meant that the wealth of the land was exported.

While there was grain and produce in Ireland, apart from potato crops, English landlords shipped grain to England to feed the cattle and though there were cattle in Ireland, English landlords shipped them to England to feed English people. Potatoes were the main crop for tenant farmers and when the crop failed in the Great Famine they were not only unable to feed their families but also they were unable to pay their rent. Landlords evicted them from their land; leaving people starving and homeless.

The Irish Rebellion of 1641 resulted in a war which continued in Ireland until the 1650s, when Oliver Cromwell's New Model Army decisively defeated the Irish and re-conquered the country.

In 1798, the Society of United Irishman embraced Catholics, Protestants, and Dissenters in its aim to remove English control from Irish affairs.

Their bloody rebellion of 1798, however, resulted in the 1801 Act of Union which brought Ireland tighter still under British control.

The Easter Rebellion in Easter week 1916 was an attempt by militant Irish Republicans to win independence from Britain. It was the most significant uprising in Ireland since the rebellion of 1798. The Rising was suppressed after six days of fighting and its leaders were executed.

The Black and Tans were mostly former soldiers brought into Ireland by the British government after 1918 to assist the Royal Irish Constabulary.

For a number of years the Royal Irish Constabulary had been a target for the Irish Republican Army. Their barracks were frequently attacked and members of the RIC were killed.

There were plenty of English ex-servicemen who were prepared to serve as Black and Tans. There were not enough uniforms for all those that had joined up. They wore a mixture of uniforms— khaki jackets and dark police uniform trousers, hence the Black and Tans. They soon acquired a reputation for brutality and their tactics have never been forgotten by the Irish people.

Notwithstanding centuries of oppression and resentment, although Ireland was neutral in World War II, it is an established fact that 70,000 citizens of neutral Ireland volunteered for the British Armed Forces together with about 30,000 citizens from Northern Ireland.

The Irish turned America into a champion of the anti-imperialist school and delayed American entry into both World Wars.

Did The Potato Famine of 1845 affect more than just Irish numbers? If it had not been for the Irish emigration to America, is it not probable that the United States would have remained largely WASP? Would Italians, Jews, Russians, Poles and other continental immigrants have been allowed entry in such numbers?

"Mass death and mass emigration following the Great Irish Potato Famine of the 1840s reduced the Irish population from almost 8.2 million in 1841 to less than 6.6 million in 1851." (Ref: The Great Irish Potato Famine, James S. Donnelly Jnr., 2001).

Without the Potato Famine would there have been a President Kennedy of the United States? Would there have been a Grace Kelly?

President Kennedy: "The most extraordinary Potato Famine descendant was John Fitzgerald Kennedy, great grand-son of Patrick Kennedy, a farmer from County Wexford who had left Ireland in 1849."

Copyright © 2000 The History Place™.

Grace Kelly: "Grace Kelly's grandfather, John Henry Kelly, was born in 1847 ('The worst year of the Irish Potato Famine') in County Mayo, Ireland. As a young man he emigrated to America and by his wife, Mary Costello, he had six sons including Grace Kelly's father, John Brendan Kelly, Snr., also known as Jack."

A Father, a Son, an American Quest, 2008, **Daniel J. Boyne**

RELIGION

Belief

Question: What does Pascal's Wager tell us about belief in God?
—G. Arnold, Nottingham

Mr. Arnold adds that he was prompted to ask about this famous argument put forward by the eponymous 17th Century French Philosopher by the recent correspondence in the *Sunday Telegraph* concerning the existence of God. Having found the arguments both for and against equally impressive, Mr. Arnold says he wondered what to believe.

First published posthumously in 1670, Pascal's argument begins with the four possibilities on offer: God's existence or non-existence, and our belief in Him, or lack of it. Pascal then attaches "pay-offs" to the resulting combinations, arguing that it is rational to choose the combination offering the biggest pay-off. For example, if God does not exist, then believing in Him means wasting a lot of time listening to boring sermons; on the other hand, if He does exist, non-believers run the risk of His wrath.

The problem, of course, is that we don't know what our chances of getting these various pay-offs actually are, as we don't know whether God exists or not (if we did, we wouldn't be going through this rigmarole in the first place). Pascal dealt with this by introducing probabilities to the various options (in the process inventing a branch of applied mathematics known today as Decision Theory). His choice of probability was, however, very much open to question. Arguing that God is as likely to exist as not, Pascal set the odds on the reality of God at 50:50. Fortunately, Pascal rendered his choice irrelevant by his further claim that belief in God combined with God actually existing produces an infinitely large pay-off—spending eternity in Heaven. He allowed Pascal to claim it is therefore rational to believe in God.

Needless to say, many see this as mathematical sleight-of-hand, and even three centuries later, a vigorous debate continues among academics about the relative merits of alternative arguments. For example, atheists have argued that the chances that God exists are precisely zero. In that case, Pascal's approach implies that belief is rational only if there is a bigger pay off from wrongly believing God exists than from correctly believing He doesn't. Atheists might say this cannot possibly be true, but the legions of happy churchgoers suggest otherwise. In any case, an insistence that the probability of God is precisely zero implies perfect knowledge, which many would argue is the preserve of…well…God. On the other hand, Pascal's approach shows that under reasonable assumptions, belief in God is rational for all who believe that they gain some benefit from such belief. Pascal's Wager is immensely rich in philosophical implications, and used judiciously can be extended to cast light even on the rationality of, say, belief in transubstantiation or reincarnation. What this ingenious mode of argument does not do is provide proof that any given belief is rational for everyone. This is because, contrary to what we are so often led to believe, such rationality is as much a matter of preference as cold logic.

Robert Matthews, *The Sunday Telegraph*, February 6, 2005

————————————

Pope John Paul II

In the spring of 1992—when I was a 29 year old Deputy Minister of Defence in Poland's first fully democratic post-war government—I was sent on a rather delicate assignment. My boss—Poland's first civilian Minister of Defence—told me to go to Rome. There I was to meet the Pope and to ask for his assistance.

It was only weeks since the Soviet Union had collapsed and everything there was up for grabs. Lech Walesa, then the President of Poland, had embarked on a harebrained scheme to acquire nuclear warheads from the former KGB. Poland, a signatory to the Nuclear Non-Proliferation Treaty would look foolish at best, a pariah at worst, if the scheme went through. Despite our efforts to talk him out of it, President Walesa seemed determined to go ahead. He is half Mahatma Gandhi, half village yokel and it was impossible ever to know which side of his personality would predominate.

On the issue of buying nuclear weapons, we felt the Pope would be the only person who could talk sense into him.

It was not difficult to arrange the meeting. Foreign dignitaries had to wait months to see the Polish Pope, but for Poles it was easier.

While in Rome at a NATO conference, I made a telephone call to a friendly priest and the following day was shown into the Pontiff's study.

I started to explain my mission—but it turned out to be unnecessary. John Paul II nodded. "I know," he said. In fact, the Vatican knew everything—about the plan, about the nukes, about the military intelligence officers who were whispering in the President's ear. The Vatican's own intelligence service was obviously sharper than ours. By the time I got back to Poland, President Walesa had already dropped talking about the plan. Karol Wojtyla had changed the history of Europe again.

My second encounter with the Pope at his summer residence in Castel Gendolfo, during the years of martial law, was more intimate. I had stayed in Britain as a political exile. The Communists took revenge on me by harassing my parents in Poland, and banning them from travel to the West.

Through the intercession of a priest relative, my parents finally obtained their passports in order to go on a pilgrimage to Rome, where they saw me and we saw the Pope together.

Before meeting the Pope face to face, you expect him to have the charisma, or at least the manner of a monarch, some quirk to indicate that this is the head of the oldest organization in the western world. The prelude before being introduced—the Vatican officials, the Swiss guards, the high vaults of the ceremonial chambers—only heighten the expectation. But John Paul II himself has the presence of a kind, old uncle who will listen to your troubles and help you out with pocket money. His is a charisma that breaks rather than erects barriers.

Audiences are highly formal occasions and the Pope usually says little, instead encouraging his visitors to talk. He asked my mother about how she managed to travel from Poland and about my studies in Britain. She broke down in tears of joy. He blessed her and handed each of us—even my father, an incorrigible agnostic—a rosary with the Papal coat of arms on the back of the cross. At this time, after two assassination attempts and a tense period in 1981—when John Paul II reportedly threatened to come to Poland if it was ever invaded by the Soviet Army—he was no longer jolly. He seemed more subdued and melancholy, as if disappointed in human nature. For us, he was the uncrowned King of Poland and we drank every word of encouragement he uttered.

The Poland in which Karol Wojtyla ascended the steps of his ecclesiastical career was indeed ruled by authoritarian, even totalitarian, regimes, first Nazi Germany and then Soviet Communism. Yet he was nurtured in opposition to them, which is why he makes such frequent and passionate pleas for respecting human rights.

Having spent three decades fighting a Communist regime, the Pope knows the power of symbolic gestures. For most of the last century, remaining personally decent, while nasty regimes came and went, was all that the average Pole could hope for. His Polishness strengthened the Pope's solidarity with the world's underdogs, hence his condemnation of Apartheid, his visit to a leper colony in the Ivory Coast, and his meal with the Vatican's tramps. His pronouncements on international relations—his belief that lasting peace can only be built on justice, may stem from his perceptions of the history of Poland.

"If you want peace, remember man," is one of his favourite maxims. Hence his advocacy of the Bosnians, the "wandering Palestinians," and the Kurds.

Radek Sikorski, *Sunday Telegraph*, February 27, 2005

—Pope John Paul II (1920–2005) became pope in 1978 and died on April 2, 2005. Radek Sikorski recalled his private meetings with the Pope and paid tribute to the personal inspiration of the man who had always fought tyranny.

On Overly Religious People

They're so heaven bound they're no earthly good.

Source Unknown

On Church Going

Once I am sure there's nothing going on,
I step inside, letting the door thud shut.
Another church: matting, seats and stone,
And little books; sprawlings of flowers, cut
For Sunday, brownish now, some brass and stuff

Up at the holy end; the small neat organ;
And a tense, musty, unignorable silence,
Brewed God knows how long. Hatless, I take off
My cycle-clips in awkward reverence.
… It pleases me to stand in silence here;
A serious house on serious earth it is,
In whose blent air all our compulsions meet.

Philip Larkin (1922–1985), English poet

REMEMBRANCE DAY

When Remembrance Day comes around my mind goes back to those I knew who are with us no more. One in particular has always stood out in my memory—Lt. Peter Wallworth.

We both trained as troopers in the Royal Armoured Corps. at Bovington Camp, Dorset, 1942–43. Although I only knew him for a very short time, he left an indelible impression on my mind and I have never forgotten him.

In fact, after Bovington I never saw him again. It was not until I went back to Holland after many years, met Luc van Gent and read his book, that I heard to my great sorrow that Peter was gone. There was another small link, in that we both came from Harrow in Middlesex.

Peter was an exceptional young man—an example for us all. Kind and easygoing, very unselfish and certainly extremely courageous.

Luc van Gent, in the course of his research, obtained some copies of correspondence including a tribute from Peter's father:

> "We are sending you a memoir as a little tribute to
> Peter. It gives a rather inadequate picture of his short
> but vivid life, but we think it may serve to preserve a
> memory which will, we hope, long be cherished
> amongst those who knew and loved him."

In memory of Peter Thomas Wallworth. The brave and precious only son of Mr. and Mrs. A. R. Wallworth:

All he had hoped for,
All he had he gave.
To save mankind,
Himself he scorned to save.

A.R.W., F.C.W., C.M.W.
(His family: father, mother and sister.)

Luc van Gent also obtained letters which Peter had sent home; some extracts follow.
After leave in January, 1943 Peter wrote:

> "Here I am again after landing with a crack into army life. Back to rough blankets, no clean soft sheets, back to dirty fingernails and constant grime, back to 'Wakey, wakey, rise and shine' at 6:30 a.m. Back to rough orders and the tramp, tramp, tramp of marching men, back to the smell of oil and petrol and the noise of these giant clanking monsters, back to the life more suited to the shaping of men than the life of soft beds, delicate foods and breath-taking girls.
> Roll on Easter (end of initial training) and then perhaps to battle—who knows! Some day we might get home to enjoy it in peace and quiet, but not yet."

September, 1944:

> "We are up half an hour before daylight and ready to move inside 15 minutes. The rest of my crew have all been wounded in Normandy and have some grim stories to tell but are grand chaps. God will guide and keep me so don't worry, but when you read or hear of armoured divisions advancing in such and such a place we shall be among the honoured few.
> I really feel that I am doing the job for which I was trained and am happy. Thank you mother for your lovely letter."

25th of October, 1944:

> "I shall certainly have tales to tell if I ever wish to recall
> incidents of the last three days. God's protection was
> proved without doubt for I am told I am extremely
> lucky to be alive. Unfortunately, I have lost all my kit
> and bedding except the spares which are somewhere
> miles behind. However, it is surprising how well one
> can get along with a piece of soap and something to eat.
> My radio operator, Hannah, was killed the other
> day…Please Mother do what you can for Mrs. Hannah
> and I will write her. We must know there is no grief
> and God is the comforter. War is no romantic
> adventure to the boys at the front. People who want to
> know why we are not advancing quicker should be told
> to come out here and try. God bless you all and pray
> for us. I often feel that you are at home thinking about
> us—keep smiling and don't worry."

In a later letter, Peter wrote:

> "I often think of you all sitting round the fire at home,
> I smile very quietly to myself—it is comforting to think
> like that. I trust life at home is reasonably normal,
> peaceful and quiet—I should hate to think it was
> different, one realizes that is the life one really loves. I
> wish we could all have leave after being in action night
> and day for over two months. I try not to cause
> unnecessary destruction and treat prisoners justly.
> Taking nothing from them other than arms, etc."

Luc van Gent obtained the name and address of Eric Lomas,
the wireless operator who was standing shoulder to shoulder in the
turret of the tank with Peter on the day it was hit. Eric Lomas replied
to a letter that I wrote and here is an extract:

> "I was not his regular operator. The reason I came to
> be on Peter's tank was that my Troop Leader at the
> time had just been sniped and killed and I had taken the

tank back on orders to clean up the inside (my Leader was shot in the neck so you can imagine what we had to clean). I was ordered back to our starting line of that day. When I reached this starting point, there was a bombed out house…and there was Peter Wallworth lying down very shaken as he had just lost his Operator. A mortar had landed on the turret and scalped his Operator. Later in the day, Peter came up to me and said I was his Operator as I was the only Troop Leader's Operator available, pack up my kit and go with him. On 8th of April, 1945 we were both in the tank with our head outside the cupola, Peter on the left, me on the right…We heard the boom of the gun. I told him I would look to my right and for him to look to his left. He nodded and that was the last thing I remember. I heard later that as we moved down the road that Sunday morning to clear out some Germans in a wood… the first boom we heard was the shell fired at the leading tank. That shell hit the road. The German elevated his gun, fired again and the shell missed the leading tank, hit a tree and then ricocheted straight onto the top of our tank turret. Peter was decapitated I was told. I had received head wounds and was unconscious."

In his letter, Eric Lomas described Peter as…"a very likeable, devoted officer to his men."

A. Michael Warrington and **Luc van Gent**, Dutch military historian

----

Holly Elementary School

Every year the teachers and students at this school in Ladner, B.C. put on a special Remembrance Day presentation consisting of songs and poems. The presentation by all of the children never fails to arouse feelings of deep emotion.

I congratulated the school principal and said that the young students were fortunate to be able to attend this kind of school. The caring teachers and the general atmosphere in the school give the impression that these children are likely to grow up to be good citizens.

A. Michael Warrington

Leave the World a Little Better

Leave the world just a little bit better.
A little better than it was.
Leave the world just a little bit better.
A little better than you found it.
When the sun came up.

I'm only one and we are two.
But there are others like me and you.
Step by step and hand in hand.
We can help our land.
Leave the world just a little bit kinder

.

A little kinder than it was.
Leave the world just a little bit kinder,
A little kinder than you found it
When the sun came up.

Charlotte Diamond, singer and songwriter. Title traced to the original phrase by **Ralph Waldo Emerson** (1803–1882), American essayist and poet, from which the song was composed in 2000.

—Sung by the children at **Holly Elementary School** at a
   Remembrance Day ceremony on November 10, 2004.

Last Night I Had The Strangest Dream

Last night I had the strangest dream,
I'd ever dreamed before.
I dreamed the world had all agreed
To put an end to war.
I dreamed I saw a mighty room,

The room was filled with men.
And the papers they were signing said
They'd never fight again.

And when the papers were all signed,
And a million copies made
They all joined hands and bowed their heads,
And grateful prayers were made.
And the people in the streets below,
They all danced round and round.
And the guns and swords and uniforms
Were scattered on the ground.

Last night I had the strangest dream,
I never dreamed before.
I dreamed the world had all agreed
to put an end to war.
I dreamed I saw a mighty room,
The room was filled with men.
And the papers they were signing said
They'd never fight again.

When I awoke, t'was but a dream,
and peace a dirty word
I tried to tell them of my dream,
But not a word they heard
And then I got me fighting mad,
And I knew just what I'd do
I'd fight nonviolently for peace,
Until my dream came true.

Ed McCurdy, composer and singer of folk music. This, his most famous song, was composed in 1950.

—Sung by the children at **Holly Elementary School** at a
   Remembrance Day ceremony on November 10, 2004

The Man We Never Knew

There's a voice that begs us to listen
And it comes from across the sea
Tho' you've never met the caller
Will you listen to his plea?
Will you pause for just a moment,
Whisper soft a prayer or two?
Will you bow your head in silence
For the man we never knew!

We know not what his name was
Nor the colour of his skin
We know not of his virtues,
Of his weaknesses, or his sins,
But we know he died in battle
Tho' he never cared for fight
For his country's call had reached him
And he died for what was right.

Was he from a teeming city,
From the village, farm or town?
Did he thrill to every sunrise,
Count his joys as night came down?
Was the breath of life sweet to him
As it is to me and you?
Was he awed by nature's wonders,
This man we never knew.

Source Unknown

—This poem was found by Rabbi M. Schector in the archives of his Royal Canadian Legion branch. Rabbi Schector is director of Chaplaincy Services at the Sir Mortimer B. Davis Jewish General Hospital, Montreal, Quebec and chaplain of the Last Post Fund and Branch No. 97, Royal Canadian Legion.

—Recited by the children at **Holly Elementary School** at a Remembrance Day ceremony on November 10, 2007.

REMORSE

Hurry up and tell me,
This is just a dream.
Oh, could we start again, please?
Could we start again?

Peter in *Jesus Christ Superstar*, a Broadway musical by **Andrew Lloyd Webber** and **Tim Rice**, 1971

SALT

Without a little salt we shall die.
I learned this in Physioloj-eye

With all the money you can muster
You can talk and shout and bluster
You can hire the greatest cooks
And read all the latest books

But—without a little salt we shall die!

A. Michael Warrington

SELF ESTEEM

I am still attracted to the things I cannot have, but I remind myself that this is not so much about getting a broken heart, but about getting a broken ego. The two can easily be confused, but it is much easier to deal with if you tell yourself it is just your ego that was broken and simply that the person did not recognize you for the wonderful person you are. It doesn't have the same depth of soul, does it, and therefore it doesn't have that same impact.

Angelica Huston, actress, on a broken relationship

_____

SETTING A GOOD EXAMPLE

If gold ruste, what shall iren do.

The Canterbury Tales, **Chaucer**

_____

While it is the job of a leader to keep his ear to the ground, it is hard for people to look up to a leader who spends too much time in that position.

Winston Churchill

_____

SEVENTH HEAVEN

If there is a seventh heaven, where are all the other six heavens?

Seventh heaven—state of blissful happiness. The Jewish religion recognises seven heavens of which the highest, the seventh, was the abode of God. The seven heavens of Islam—the seventh being a place of divine light and pure ecstasy—come from this. The division was of Babylonian origin, founded on astronomical theories. Despite this antiquity the expression was not used in its modern secular sense until the 19th century, probably as a result of increased British familiarity with Islam during the period of the British Empire. According to the Islamic concept of heaven, one goes after death to the heaven he or she has earned on earth, and the seventh heaven, ruled by Abraham, is the ultimate one, a region of pure light, lying above the other six, the heaven of heavens.

Source Unknown

Thinking about Seven Heavens makes one wonder. If one "just makes it" into the first heaven—and a lot of your friends and relatives are in different heavens—can you ever get to "graduate" to higher heavens? Of, if not, can you get a "Day Pass" to visit some of the other heavens—presuming you know where the others are, if they are not with you?

Source Unknown

SHAKESPEARE

What's done cannot be undone.

Macbeth

Who dares not stir by day must walk by night.

King John

Wisely and slow. They stumble that run fast.

Romeo and Juliet

All the world's a stage,
And all the men and women merely players.
They have their exits and their entrances.
And one man in his time plays many parts,
His acts being seven ages. At first, the infant,
Mewling and puking in the nurse's arms.
Then the whining school boy, with his satchel
And shining morning face, creeping like snail
Unwillingly to school. And then the lover,
Sighing like furnace, with a woeful ballad
Made to his mistress' eyebrow. Then a soldier,
Full of strange oaths and bearded like the pard,
Jealous in honour, sudden and quick in quarrel,
Seeking the bubble reputation
Even in the cannon's mouth. And then the justice,
In fair round belly with good capon lined,
With eyes severe and beard of formal cut,
Full of wise saws and modern instances;

And so he plays his part. The sixth age shifts,
Into the lean and slippered pantaloon,
With spectacles on nose and pouch on side;
His youthful hose, well saved, a world too wide
For his shrunk shank, and his big manly voice,
Turning again towards childish treble pipes
And whistles in his sound. Last scene of all,
That ends this strange eventful history,
Is second childishness and mere oblivion,
Sans teeth, sans eyes, sans taste, sans everything.

As You Like It

Love is blind, and lovers cannot see.
The pretty follies that themselves commit.

The Merchant of Venice

How sharper than a serpent's tooth it is
To have a thankless child.

King Lear

He must have a long spoon that must eat with the Devil.

The Comedy of Errors

I must go and meet with danger there,
Or it will seek me in another place
And find me worse provided.

Henry IV

Cowards die many times before their deaths;
The valiant never taste of death but once.

Julius Caesar

There is a tide in the affairs of men
Which, taken at the flood, leads onto fortune;
Omitted, all the voyage of their life
Is bound in shallows and in miseries.
On such a fool sea are we now afloat,
And we must take the current when it serves,
Or lose our ventures.

Julius Caesar

This day is called the Feast of Crispian:
He that outlives this day, and comes safe home,
Will stand a-tip toe when this day is named,
And rouse him at the name of Crispian.

And we few, we happy few, we band of brothers;
For he today that sheds his blood with me
Shall be my brother.

And gentlemen in England, now abed,
Shall think themselves accursed they were not here;
And hold their manhoods cheap whiles any speaks
That fought with us upon St. Crispin's Day.

Henry V

—The young King, age 27, rousing the English army going into the
  battle of Agincourt. The English, with some 6,000 men, were facing
  an army of about 25,000.

What's gone, and what's past help, should be past grief.

The Winter's Tale

A good leg will fall;
A straight back will stoop;
A black beard will turn white;
A curled pate will grow bald;
A fair face will wither;
A full eye will wax hollow:
But a good heart, Kate, is the sun and the moon;
Or, rather, the sun and not the moon;
For it shines bright and never changes.

Henry IV

SHORT STORIES

<u>What If...</u>

Sniff, sniff. "Do you know what I heard today?"

Sniff, sniff. "No. What?"

"Your folk are going to emigrate and they're not taking you with them!"

"Where's Emigrate?"

"It's not a place. It's something I learned at Hound U. Emigrate means leave the country and they want you...they want you to..." (He growled softly, cast his eyes downward and looked away.) "It's hard to say this and all the canines are very upset—we had a big meeting this morning before you were let out."

"What? What? What is it?"

"If they can't find a good home—and they're hard to find—they'll arrange for you to go to that Big Kennel in the Sky."

"What?!"

He sat down and scratched his ear thoughtfully..."Well, nobody's ever come back to tell us, but they say once you pass the Dog's Judgement Day there are unlimited bones forever, it's never cold or wet and there's a never-ending supply of members of the opposite sex."

"Well, that doesn't sound too bad, but what if you don't pass the Dog's Judgement Day?"

"Then you go to a place called Hell—it's full of pit bull terriers doing life for killing people."

"But I've never killed anyone!"

"I know, I know—but there is a kind of a halfway house where you serve your time for all the minor things like bringing home dead rats and messing on the carpet—but wait, we had an idea."

"What's that?" (He pricked up his ears and looked at his friend very attentively.)

"All of us canines decided to form a union—the Beneficial Association of Registered Canines, or BARC for short."

"What good will that do?"

"We're going to lose control of our bladders all day, and we're going to imagine we hear burglars and bark all night, and our owners will get so mad at your family that they'll have to change their minds and take you with them."

"Gee, that's great!" He sneezed with excitement and wagged his tail vigorously. "Buster, you're a pal—let's hope it works, and will you thank the guys for me?"

Buster got up and stretched. "Sure will." (Big confident bark.) "Us dogs have to stick together—united we stand but divided we go to that horrible vet." He scraped and pawed the ground, put his mark on the nearby fire hydrant and loped off down the road.

"Thanks, Buster."

A. Michael Warrington

<u>The Demon</u>

The demon walks along the red embers with jaded boredom…at least he tries to will himself to be jaded and bored. Things have been rather dull in demon land of late since they developed this vaccine against demonic possession. There are now thousands of demons trying to get in. Pretty soon the big demons are going to start demonizing the little demons—and there'll always be a bigger demon than yourself, even if you do pump yourself up with demonoid juice (which they say can wreck your liver, not to mention shrink your reproductive parts and make your voice squeaky.)

So, it's not fun anymore being a demon. And here he is having been sold a bill of goods—that if you walk on hot coals you can get to do anything. It's all a matter of building your confidence—don't think about hot coals, just think "I'm the BEST!" But act casual—make

haste slowly as you singe your way across the glowing embers—and if you don't immediately start finding and working on likely prospects to demonize, you can always make a living by franchising the idea to all the other failed demons—and so on ad infinitum…

A. Michael Warrington

The Artist

The artist I knew in our small town was an untidy fellow, with long hair and a beard that always looked as though it needed to be combed. He lived by himself and was indulged rather than liked by the local people.

Every so often he would persuade the community hall to put on a showing of his works, of which he produced a great variety of different subjects—ships, country scenes and the occasional nude.

He was prolific rather than talented, and no one knew how he managed to survive—certainly his art did not keep him. He rarely sold more than one or two pieces at his showings, and he invariably ended up giving the rest away to anyone who showed the slightest interest.

He had just appeared one day about ten years ago and rented a small cottage with a large, airy attic on the outskirts of town. He was extremely thin, made no friends and was the object of curiosity and intrigue, provoking speculation as to his origin.

He received little mail and, apart from his occasional foray to buy food and his periodic showings, remained a man of mystery. For all I knew he was still there minding his own business, with everyone still wondering who he was and where he had come from.

The mystery was to be solved for me some years later by the strangest coincidence.

A. Michael Warrington

The General Store

It was a small general store with a post office inside, set back a little way from the road with space for cars to park and a fence, with posters and placards advertising local events, separating it from the next lot.

A Honda Accord drove up and a woman got out. She glanced around once, then walked easily over to the store and went in.

It was a typical sort of place with shelves of dry goods, newspaper and magazine racks and a large freezer with the milk and ice cream. At the front was a counter and cash register with a pleasant faced young woman serving a customer. At the back was another counter with a big sign saying "POST OFFICE." Behind that counter was a slim, wiry man of late middle age wearing a shirt with short sleeves rolled up, a nondescript tie and a waistcoat. He looked up with a bright, inquisitive "Now who might this be" expression, since he knew just about everyone and everything in this small town.

She was a woman in her mid-thirties with an easy manner—fair hair casually groomed, generous figure, well proportioned but not plump, blue sweater, skirt and comfortable but expensive looking shoes. Her face had a lived-in look, expressive, not excessively lined, with a calm, direct gaze—a woman whom one would say had been around and seen and done a lot but without visible scars.

The postmaster, who had looked down to busy himself with a drawer after his first scrutiny, now looked up as she approached. "I'm looking for someone who I believe lives in this town and I wonder if you might know him."

His face became animated—he loved showing off his knowledge and he couldn't help but be curious about this newcomer.

"Well, I was born not far from here and I've been here 20 years, so who might you be looking for?"

"It's someone I used to know a long time ago. I heard he moved here maybe 10 or 12 years ago…" Her voice trailed off.

"What was his name?"

"Cleghorn—Jim Cleghorn."

"Oh, I know him—he's our resident artist. He often puts on showings—he's part of our local culture." He grinned.

She paused for a while and studied the man behind the counter. He had bright blue eyes, and fair hair growing thin. He also had fair hair sprouting from both nostrils and both ears, and even a small tuft growing from the surface of the middle of his nose. Strange, she thought. I wonder why he doesn't do his nose while he's shaving?

She spoke again slowly—"Can you tell me where he lives?"

"Sure can—he rents a place from my sister-in-law—been there about 10 years. But he has no phone—you would just have to go around there." His eyes sparkled.

"Thank you—if you can just tell me where he lives. Oh, and if you can recommend somewhere to eat—I've come a long way—I'll just have some lunch and then go around there this afternoon."

He quickly sized her up again, "You wouldn't want to go to the Elite Café—that's where the locals drop in for coffee and a smoke—you could go to the motel. My son runs it with his wife—Dave and Hilda—they have a nice little restaurant. I'll give them a ring if you'll tell me your name." He looked at her expectantly.

"Well, thank you—but I think I'll just go round there, if you don't mind." She didn't want everyone to know her name—at least not yet.

He tried not to show his disappointment as she let herself out and the door closed behind her.

It was a typical motel and restaurant set back a bit from the road, with a cream stucco exterior and green trim. There were a few cars parked in the spaces reserved for the units and it looked a comfortable sort of a place in the warm afternoon sunshine.

She chose a table by a window where she could look out and watch the few cars driving by—mostly summer tourists looking for the hunting and fishing resorts further up the valley.

As she waited for a menu, her mind went back over the years, as it had so many times over the last few months, and she asked herself what she was doing here and why had she come?

After all, the events which refused to fade from her memory had taken place a long time ago. But, with an anxious little shiver of anticipation, she realized it was something she had to do.

A. Michael Warrington

<u>The Bank</u>

Waskena was a small prairie town (population 350) with a bank, a pharmacy, a hotel and the usual assortment of small businesses and shops fronting the one main street. The reeve, or mayor as he preferred to be called, was named Lorne McGregor, and he was generally held in high regard, which he himself would be the first to acknowledge. In fact, it took little more than a casual perusal to note that the pharmacy was called McGregor's Pharmacy, the hotel was McGregor's Hotel, the garage with one gas pump and a service bay was

McGregor's Garage and the store was McGregor's General Store. In fact, while the bank was the Toronto Dominion, it was widely known and accepted that if you needed a loan you had better be on good terms with the manager, who happened to be McGregor's son-in-law.

One particular night, around midnight, a call came through to the RCMP detachment, which was located in the next town some 10 miles along the highway to the east. The call was taken by the sole Mountie, Constable Jim Cleghorn, a veteran of some years standing.

It was the manager of the Waskena bank saying someone had spotted movement inside the bank and could he come at once.

Jim quickly got dressed and strapped on his belt, holster and sidearm. He was a man of well-above-average height and a lean and rangy build, with cool grey eyes and the kind of weather tanned countenance one acquired from years on the prairies. Right now he was in a great hurry. He went outside, got into the patrol car and roared off down the highway. In this part of the province it was still a gravel highway, but okay as long as you kept off the shoulders, and he knew the road very well.

Approaching the Waskena bank, he cut his motor, switched off his lights and rolled silently to a halt as Lorne McGregor's son-in-law, the bank manager, stepped out of the shadows and addressed him quietly.

"I don't know what's going on, Jim. It looks as though there's someone in the bank."

"Nobody cleaning up at this time?" asked Jim.

"No—the cleaner's always done and gone by eight. I don't understand it—the alarm hasn't gone off. The druggist was getting some painkillers for the Robinson kid—he had a toothache—and he said he saw movement inside the bank and he called me. It's dark, but with the moonlight, it's not dark enough."

"Do you have a key to the front door, and is there a door at the back?"

"Yes, we can get in both ways."

"OK—you go quietly in by the front and give me the key to get in the back and…"

"Well, there's two keys to the back—one for the regular lock and one for the deadbolt—here."

"OK, we'll both count slowly to 30. That'll give me time to get around to the back door. Then we'll go in at the same time and we'll catch whoever's in there."

The idea that someone was prowling around inside his bank was enough to subdue any natural fears the bank manager might have had, and the fact that he had an armed officer of the law with him boosted his confidence. With a sense of excitement and adventure, he began counting. He could see the headlines in the local paper: "Bank Manager Captures Thief."

"...27, 28, 29, 30."

Officer Cleghorn inserted the two keys into the locks one after the other, cursing the faint clicks as the bolt slid back. He quickly stepped inside, closing the door quietly behind him. He stood with drawn revolver and flashlight ready, every sense alert, straining his eyes in the darkness. He heard a faint creaking from the front of the bank. Then there was complete silence. For a minute or so nothing happened.

"Police!" Officer Cleghorn's sudden shout broke the stillness. He switched on his flashlight, holding it out away from his body. "Come towards me with your hands up!"

Suddenly there was a clatter as a chair was knocked over, sounds of stampeding feet, confused shouts and cries.

By the light of his flashlight, the Mountie saw two figures struggling on the floor—one got up and came hurtling towards him. "STOP RIGHT THERE OR I'LL SHOOT!"

The figure cannoned into the policeman, knocking the flashlight out of his hand as his gun went off.

A strangled cry came from the front of the bank. The fugitive crashed through the back door and vanished as the Mountie groped for his light, filled with a sickening dread. Had the bank manager been hit? He had to find out. He went forward and kneeled beside him. The flashlight confirmed his worst fear—the bank manager had been hit in the throat and was bleeding copiously. Eyes staring, he shuddered convulsively, made a choking, gurgling sound and lay still.

"Dear God, no!"

With a surge of adrenaline the Mountie stormed out of the back door, looked and listened. He stood for a while, realizing that his chance of finding the fugitive were receding with every second. Lights came on in the next building and a door opened just as he heard a car start up. Shouting to the neighbour to send for the doctor, he ran to his car and accelerated wildly, just in time to see a convertible turning for the highway.

Filled with a cold fury, he gave chase. Swerving onto the

highway, he gunned the engine in hot pursuit, cursing the clouds of dust which partly obscured the car ahead.

With grim satisfaction he found himself closing in, closer…closer. As he drew nearer, the other car began to barrel and sway from side to side to block him from overtaking.

"All right, you bastard! I'll stay behind you till I get you."

The two cars hurtled through the quiet prairie night. As they came to a bend the runaway slithered onto the soft shoulder, skidding along with two wheels down as the driver frantically tried to power himself back onto the road. The car bucked violently up and down and then, with it's engine screaming, shot off the road, somersaulted several times and shuddered along on its roof before finally coming to rest.

Officer Cleghorn climbed out of his car and surveyed the scene with his flashlight.

The car was a mangled wreck and 10 yards away was the driver. He recognized him—a teller from the bank, Rod Smith. Recently divorced, he was under threat of suspension for unpaid debts. He was beyond all threat of suspension now. One leg was bent under him at an odd angle, his head was crushed on one side and an eyeball was protruding from its socket. He was quite dead.

Officer Cleghorn turned around and drove back to town.

He felt chilled and had a sick feeling in his stomach. He would have to try to explain to the relatives how a routine call had turned into a nightmare. He went over the S.O.P.s in his mind: *Do not unholster your personal weapon unless danger is imminent. Do not use deadly force unless your life is in danger and do not fire without warning.*

But he hadn't meant to shoot, it was a total accident. What should he have done differently?

There would be a police inquiry and a coroner's inquest.

It was a thoroughly bad situation but just how bad was more than he could foresee at that time.

A. Michael Warrington

<u>The Quest</u>

It was easy to find the address provided by the postmaster at the general store—a cottage more than a house, with a garden in front, separated from the road by a small picket fence, and with a gravel path leading up to the front door.

Knowing that he would not be expecting visitors, least of all someone from times long gone by, she felt her pulse accelerating—her usual calm having left her back at the motel when she sat contemplating this next step in her quest.

There was a bell beside the sun-faded front door. She pressed it and waited. She pressed it again. No answer. She didn't know whether to be relieved or disappointed, but summoning her resolve to see it through, she pressed the bell again and again.

Finally, she heard movement from somewhere within and then the sound of a bolt being pulled back. At length the door opened a couple of inches and she found herself looking into the eyes of the man she had long given up on ever seeing again. The eyes were the same—intelligent, grey eyes that used to make her heart turn over and, she realized now as the memories came flooding back, still did.

He looked at her suspiciously.

"What do you want?"

"Jim?—Jim Cleghorn? Don't you remember me?"

He studied her. "No. Should I?"

"Jim—I'm Maureen. Maureen Turner—you and my brother were best friends…" she paused "…a long time ago."

His eyes changed and a puzzled expression replaced the look of distrust as he stared at her.

"Aren't you going to ask me in?"

Wordlessly he opened the door and stood aside.

She crossed the threshold and found herself in a sitting room, with a table and a couple of chairs at one end, and an opening leading into a small kitchen and eating nook. There was a narrow stairway up from the hall. He stood awkwardly, looking at her.

"Jim," she said, quietly and tenderly, "it's been so long—I just knew one day I had to try and find you."

He didn't answer. The way he stood, just looking at her—the great change she saw in him, the straggly beard, the painful thinness—

so unlike the virile, strong, confident man she had once known. Now… this almost frail, vulnerable…she felt a wave of pity and compassion, sensing all he must have gone through.

"Can I sit down?"

He seemed to shake himself and gestured towards a chair. She felt embarrassed now, realizing how he must feel at having his privacy invaded.

She sat down facing him while he pulled over another chair.

So this was Maureen Turner—a chapter from his life that he had tried to forget. She was an elegant woman, radiating health, with an easy, graceful manner. She looked calmly at him with a gentle, reassuring smile—all of her previous apprehension now gone.

"Jim…"

"Mo, you shouldn't have come…I don't know what to say to you…It's best to leave things as they are…I don't know what to say…"

"Jim, don't say anything—I'm just so glad to see you! Can we just have a cup of coffee? You don't have to say anything. I know things now that you don't know. Please—can't I just stay a while? It's so good to see you again."

It distressed her to see his threadbare pants and the holes in the elbows of his sweater. As he poured water into the kettle, she looked around and noted the faded carpets, the sparse, well-worn furniture and the walls lined with dusty pictures and paintings.

For the next two hours he hardly said a word as she went over the intervening years.

"You know Jim—you were the love of my life, but you were so much older than me, I could never tell you. When you used to come over in that old car to pick up Brad, I hoped you'd look at me, even just to say hello." He flinched and looked away.

She sensed his embarrassment and went on. "I understand how you feel—I know, we knew, what you went through. The mayor blamed you for shooting his son-in-law. He turned the whole town against you and it went all through the province."

"Killer cop," he said quietly and bitterly. "I'll never forget. The inquiry was bad enough. But then a reprimand for 'careless use of a firearm' when it was just an accident—I couldn't live with the accusation. Everywhere I went—everyone knew. Everyone believed the mayor. So I asked for my release and they let me go with a small pension for my years of service. I just left and got away as far as I could. I travelled around from place to place for a few years and finally came here where nobody knew anything about me."

"But you know, Jim, the mayor died five years ago and he had such a hold on that town. It's still just a small prairie town. Brad goes there often—he's in the grain shipping business. He knows all the farmers and he often stays in the hotel. There's been a big change in how people look at things. They felt kind of relieved when the mayor died. It's as though they're all living their own lives now. They've talked amongst themselves and the people who knew you well have spoken up. Many people now believe what was said at the inquest—that you were hit in the dark and your gun went off accidentally. More and more people see it that way—that you weren't the type to shoot because you were scared or nervous. It was, just as you said, an accident."

"Well," he said looking at her now, "even if all of that is true—it's too late. My life has changed—I'm here now, and here I'm going to stay." She felt a pang and knew that she could never leave things like this.

"Jim, I want to tell you a little bit about myself. Remember the farm? Well, Dad still tries to do everything himself, but he can't do it anymore. Brad is just not interested in taking over, and I have my own career." She felt the words coming in a rush—slow down, slow down, not all at once.

She continued more calmly, reminding him about the days when he and Brad had helped with the seeding in the spring and the harvesting in the fall. Even then, Jim the teenager had been strong, tall, wiry and a hard worker—full of life and fun. He enjoyed the farm and always said that if he couldn't be a Mountie, he'd be a farmer. But Brad, her brother, the quiet, thoughtful one, said he'd work smarter, not harder—let the others break their backs. Those long summer days were wonderful, remember? It seemed they'd never end.

The boys grew up. She recalled how Jim was accepted for the Mounties—just the type they were looking for—and went to boot camp in Regina. Brad went to agricultural college. Mo took languages at university, went into investment banking—Zurich and Frankfurt—and now had a job with a major bank. Some relationships, nothing permanent.

She spoke quietly and earnestly on into the evening.

He began to relax a little as he listened to her soft voice. His mind returned to the summers of his youth—his best friend Brad and Brad's younger sister, Mo, who was now here sitting in front of him.

She was a kid then, but bright and pretty with a captivating, impish personality. He had noticed her but feigned indifference.

She felt a warm glow. Why not go back to his roots and forget all the bad things that had happened? Take up the work he used to love. The changing rhythm of the seasons; the hard physical labour, the cold prairie winters, deep snow and utter stillness, the hot dry summers and always the challenge of the harvest. Her dad used to say, "It's always been next year's country. People in a hurry just move on."

Yes, it could work, and after that—well, who knows, things might just fall into place.

"Would there be another cup of coffee in that pot, Jim?"

A. Michael Warrington

<u>Lost Summers</u>

I knew Mo Turner first of all as one of the women who worked in the bank where I spent my working days. Sometimes we met at seminars on investment banking and once there was a trip to Europe dealing with all the ramifications of a consortium involving our bank

There was something about her that fascinated me. Perhaps it was her calm manner—her poise in the rather frenetic world we shared. Or maybe the fact that she was outstandingly attractive—not in the pin-up sense, but certainly in a way that made most men give her more than a passing look.

Since I had gone through a soul searing divorce I had been wary of further involvements and felt fortunate that at least there had been no children during that short and stormy relationship.

Having grown up in a small town in B.C., I still went back from Toronto to my home province for family gatherings and occasional skiing holidays. I gradually came to know Mo Turner better and felt it was my luck and good fortune that, while there was always a certain reserve, she seemed to have time for me—and didn't seem to mind my attempts to engage her in conversation at every available opportunity.

By chance one day I had mentioned where I grew up. She looked almost startled for a moment and said: "I know that place—or I knew someone that lived there."

"Who was that?" I asked.

"His name was Jim Cleghorn."

The name was vaguely familiar. "What did he do there?" I asked. "I knew pretty well everyone but don't seem to know that name, and yet it does ring a faint bell."

"Well, he didn't come from there or grow up there. He was an artist and he lived in a small cottage on the outskirts of town."

I knew who she meant—the artist—a man of mystery. No one knew who he really was or where he came from.

"How did you know him—did he come from B.C.?"

"No, I grew up on the Prairies." She stopped and looked down, pensively. I waited, hoping she'd go on.

After a few moments she looked up, a little sadly I thought. "Maybe one day I'll tell you about it. Right now we have got to get back to work…"

I couldn't get this extraordinary coincidence out of my mind. It was intriguing. Who was Jim Cleghorn and what possible connection could there be between him and this lovely woman? I found myself thinking about her constantly, and the fact that we worked at the same institution meant that I saw her frequently. When I wasn't fully occupied with the frantic pace of volatile emerging markets, foreign loans, bond rates, mergers, acquisitions and the state of the U.S. Federal Reserve Board, she was always in my thoughts. I used to look for the next opportunity to meet, as if by chance—sometimes going out of my way to do so.

At a seminar one day we had lunch together and as the afternoon was free time we went for a walk. It was a beautiful day in late spring. We strolled in a nearby park, finding a bench near a pond with overhanging willow trees. There was a woman nearby with two small children who were busy feeding the ducks. It was quiet and peaceful and we relaxed in the warm sunshine.

Thinking this might be an opportune time, I could contain my curiosity no longer: "You know, it's extraordinary that you knew the town where I grew up—I can't help wondering what brought you there…" I hesitated and looked at her.

She glanced at me and slowly began to talk. "I grew up on the Prairies—on a farm—quite a big one, by prairie standards that is—two sections. My father used to run it himself with help from my brother and me at seeding and harvesting time—that is when I was old enough to help. The farm's still there but Dad's retired. He manages the best he can with hired help. My brother never wanted to work on the farm—he used to say 'Let others break their backs.'" She smiled and continued.

"There was a fellow who used to come over all the time—my brother's best friend—Jim Cleghorn. They always went around together and I had I suppose what you'd call a crush on Jim. He was lots of fun and maybe a bit wild but he loved helping on the farm and I loved seeing him though I was a lot younger and he never took any notice of me." She smiled again, a little ruefully I thought, and then she went on.

"I used to look forward to those long, hot summers—it meant that Jim would practically live at our place. Everyone was out all day in the sunshine. We got beautifully tanned and healthy-looking. The boys used to have such fun together, always kidding around. I was just the kid sister but I pretty well adored Jim Cleghorn. I used to wish those summers would never end. Anyway, Jim was finally old enough to join the Mounties and after a couple of moves he was posted to a small town in Saskatchewan. He was the only policeman in a patch of 500 square miles—two small towns and a lot of scattered farms and settlements."

Mo paused for a few moments and then went quietly on.

She told me how everything was fine until when Jim answered a call to the bank late one night and the bank manager was accidentally shot and killed. The mayor blamed Jim, labelled him a killer cop, spread the word through the whole province and ruined his career. Jim took retirement with a small pension and went far away. Mo could never get over what happened and made up her mind that one day if she ever had the time she would try to find him. She finally tracked him down in my own home town—the artist no one really knew. So that was the connection.

Then she had the great idea that so much time had gone by, the mayor had died, most people had got on with their lives and, even though it had been all over the province, people had since taken a more realistic view. Why shouldn't he go back to work on her dad's farm, and then, well, who knows?

"And did he go back?" I asked.

"Yes…yes, he did. I had to talk him into it and go back and visit two or three times before he finally agreed."

Her dad was glad to see Jim; he had always liked him and Jim seemed to settle into the work. However, he was moody, irritable and suspicious—especially if anyone came to call, which happens often on the prairies. He had a room in the house, and when he wasn't out working, apart from meals which he shared with Mo's dad, he used to just stay in his room. He used to do a bit of hunting but seemed to have no other interests.

"We all hoped things would improve as time went by, and I went back as often as I could to try and cheer him up. He seemed to try and brighten up when I went to visit but things never really got any better, and one day...one day he didn't come in for supper and Dad went looking for him. He found him by the tractor..."—her voice broke—"He had killed himself with a shotgun." Her eyes slowly filled with tears. "Why, why, why? I keep asking myself. Why? Why couldn't he have settled down? It could have been great for him."

The sight of her tears moved me profoundly. Her usual quiet strength had evaporated and the look of anguish on her face made me want to take her in my arms.

I didn't know what to say and we sat silently for a little while.

As she touched her eyes with a tissue, I placed my hand on hers and said: "I'm sorry."

"He left a note addressed to me—I still carry it around with me." She took a piece of paper out of her wallet and passed it to me.

Dearest Mo,

Thank you for trying. The summers you used to talk about were another lifetime—gone and lost forever. It's no good anymore. I'm sorry I couldn't return the love you gave me. Thank your dad. Forgive me, Mo.

Love, Jim

I tried to comfort her. I realized now that I loved his woman and I would always want to be near her. Part of the vanity of being a man is that we always want to be a woman's first love. I knew this would never be—but there did seem to be something between us.

I looked back at my disastrous marriage—nothing as traumatic as what Mo had gone through. She seemed to gather herself again and put the note back in her wallet.

"I keep telling myself what's passed is past, and I can't keep this grieving place in my mind forever—I'm lucky to have my work."

To my enormous relief she smiled and seemed to brighten again.

This was not the occasion but maybe I could let her know at the right time how I felt about her.

I remembered some lines from a poem:

Better by far you should forget and smile.
Than that you should remember and be sad.

It was not her fault things ended that way. After all, she had done her best to help. Jim was not a happy man living the life of a recluse in my home town. Things don't always turn out the way we plan. Better to remember the good times and forget the rest—life goes on.

As we walked back into town, I think we both felt that sharing this part of her life had drawn us closer.

Although we didn't know it at the time, there would be many occasions in the years to come when we would look back on that warm afternoon in the park as the real beginning of our new life together—and it was the artist who settled in my home town, the man of mystery, whose life in the end was to form part of the pattern which shaped our destiny.

A. Michael Warrington

Rivalry

As the good-looking young waiter approached to take another order, the older waitress fretted in the corner of the hotel restaurant. "When will they ever realize that looks are only skin deep? The women sit covertly admiring his trim rear as he weaves his way between the tables. Do they ever wonder if he has washed his hands, for example. Sure he has flashy white teeth and the white shirt sets off his tan—but is he clean? Is he really CLEAN?"

You can tell the men don't like him: Why doesn't he get a real job?"

He says he is saving up to go to university, but he has been here a couple of years now and he is taking the bread and butter out of my mouth. His customers get all the best tables—the ones by the window—and mine get the tables by the kitchen and the washroom. And because my customers don't like their tables they take it out on me, as though it's my fault that they're in a constant draught from people rushing by. Well, I wasn't always old and not good to look at. When I was young, well, sure I was no Marilyn Monroe, but I had a good figure, which used to draw some appreciative looks, and my face was pleasant, if not particularly good looking, before I got slightly wrinkled with a sagging chin and baggy eyes."

But what the heck. I know more about the tricks of the trade than he'll ever know. When the veal is off, I tell 'em that the salmon's fresh in from the ocean (how will they know it's farmed salmon?)."

And the steak—why it was still on the hoof the day before yesterday—and when we're out of *Châteauneuf-du-Pape*, I just take the old empty bottle and fill it up with *Vin Ordinaire* and they think it's the real thing. They're always wanting me to pitch in and help in the kitchen, and sometimes in the back office, without giving me a raise or even a thank you."

Just then the boss came up to her. "Betty, the restaurant manager has just told me he's quitting, like, now. He has to go back east—family reasons. I need a hotel manager. You've been pinch-hitting here for years now. You know all the ropes. You won't need that waitress uniform anymore. There's no time to find another manager. I'll give you a clothing allowance, a hair salon appointment every month and triple your salary for starters. Would you do it?"

"Would I—do birds fly?" And she added under her breath, "I always did say virtue brings its own reward."

A. Michael Warrington

A Teacher's Lot

Jonathan braced himself before going to the classroom to face his motley collection of students, girls and boys, the products of a permissive age.

Well, maybe you could hardly blame them.

His eyes surveyed the room as they more or less settled into a state of sloppy preparedness for the day's lessons.

There was Stanley—a large, ungainly youth with two rings in each ear, a ring in his right nostril, head completely shaved with the exception of a coconut tuft on top, dyed bright green.

Glenda sat directly in front, a busty, blonde girl, very aware of her physical attributes and the effect she had on the young males around her. She had a tattoo above the right ankle and one just visible at the top of her left chest.

At least she had a sense of humour unlike Kaylee, who occupied a seat in the back row with her hand cupping her chin while she glowered.

Then there was Syd, the problem boy.

Jonathan got Syd in exchange for another problem boy, only Syd was worse. The other school had said, "We'll take your problem, if you'll take one of ours." So, he got Syd.

Syd wrote the book on disruptiveness. He didn't shout or fight or throw things around, he just never stopped talking or asking questions—that and his loud laugh. He was a Special Needs if ever there was one but there were just not enough Special Needs teachers to go around. Meanwhile, this one student seemed to need 75 percent of Jonathan's attention, which was not fair on the rest of the class. Most of them came from single-parent families.

Today Dale was missing.

"Where is Dale—does anyone know?" asked Jonathan.

Syd's high-pitched whine cut across the class. "Dale's making teenager movies for his uncle. He gets paid for doing weird things!"

Another typical day.

Well, when I've stuck it out with Syd as long as I can—they'll demand a minimum of three months—I'll lobby the principal every day till we can get him transferred. But then—and it's a big but—what kind of a problem will we get in exchange?

Jonathan felt his stomach muscles tighten and he braced himself once more for another day in his classroom in the city core.

A. Michael Warrington

SILENCE

You need silence to listen to your ghosts.

BBC mini-series *Oliver's Travels* (1995), **Alan Bates**

SLOW TWITCH, QUICK TWITCH

Attending Secondary School in England in 1936 I found I was good at running. On the Annual Sports Day, aged 12, I entered the 100 yard race. Next to me at the start was a short, little Irishman named Dermot Grace. I thought, "I'll easily beat you." How mistaken I was. His little legs went like pistons and he came in an easy first. In the cross country runs (5 miles), however, I came in first every time.

It was many, many years later that I found out why.

Skeletal muscles are made up of bundles of individual muscle fibres consisting of two main types—slow twitch and quick twitch. Slow twitch fibres use oxygen more efficiently to generate more fuel (known as Adenosine Triphosphate or ATP) for continuous muscle contractions over a long time. They fire more slowly than quick twitch and can go for a long time before they fatigue.

Quick twitch fibres fire more rapidly and are better at generating short bursts of speed but they fatigue more quickly.

The proportion of slow twitch and quick twitch fibres that a person has in their skeletal muscle determines whether they will be better at quick sprints or long distance running.

A. Michael Warrington

SO MUCH TO DO

So little time—so much to do.

Cecil Rhodes (1853–1902)

—Rhodes was a statesman and Empire builder, and was Prime Minster of the Colony of South Africa. He went to South Africa in 1870 to be a farmer with his brother. He obtained a degree from Oxford University and became a diamond miner in South Africa. He established the De Beers Consolidated Mines Limited. By 1891, the company owned 90 percent of the world's diamond mines. The area now known as Zimbabwe and Zambia were formerly known as Rhodesia—named after him. His business endeavours made him very wealthy. He left most of his wealth to Oxford University. The nearly 3 million pounds were used in the creation of the famous Rhodes Scholarship.

SONGS

<u>Galway Bay</u>

If you ever go across the sea to Ireland,
Then maybe at the closing of your day.
You will sit and watch the moon rise over Claddagh,
And see the sun go down on Galway Bay.

Just to hear again the ripple of the trout stream,
The women in the meadows making hay,
And to sit beside a turf fire in the cabin,
And to watch the barefoot Gossoons at their play.

For the breezes blowing o'er the seas from Ireland,
Are perfumed by the heather as they blow,

And the women in the uplands diggin' pratties,
Speak a language that the strangers do not know.

For the strangers came and tried to teach us their way,
They scorn'd us just for being what we are,
But they might as well go chasing after moonbeams,
Or light a penny candle from a star.

And if there is going to a life hereafter,
And somehow I am sure there's going to be,
I will ask my God to let me make my heaven,
In that dear land across the Irish Sea.

Written by **Dr. Arthur Colahan** (1884–1952) in 1927

_____

The Kerry Dancers

Oh, the days of the Kerry dancing
Oh, the ring of the piper's tune
Oh, for one of those hours of gladness
Gone, alas, like our youth, too soon!

When the boys began to gather
In the glen of a summer's night
And the Kerry piper's tuning
Made us long with wild delight!
Oh, to think of it
Oh, to dream of it
Fills my heart with tears!

James Lyman Molloy (1837–1909), composer and lyricist

_____

Buttons and Bows

East is east and west is west
And the wrong one I have chose
Let's go where I'll keep on wearin'
Those frills and flowers and buttons and bows

Rings and things and buttons and bows

Don't bury me in this prairie
Take me where the cement grows
Let's move down to some big town
Where they love a gal by the cut o' her clothes
And I'll stand out
In buttons and bows

I'll love you in buckskin
Or skirts that I've homespun
But I'll love ya' longer, stronger where
Yer friends don't tote a gun

My bones denounce
The buckboard bounce,
And the cactus hurts my toes.
Let's vamoose where gals keep usin'
Those silks and satins and linen that shows.
And I'm all yours
In buttons and bows

Gimme eastern trimmin'
Where women are women
In high silk hose and peek-a-boo clothes
And French perfume,
That rocks the room
And I'm all yours
In buttons and bows.

Music by **Jay Livingston**, lyrics by **Ray Evans**, 1947

—The song appeared in the 1948 movie *The Paleface* with Bob Hope
   and Jane Russell.

———————————

The Village of St. Bernadette

I've travelled far, the land and the sea
Beautiful places I happened to be

One little town I'll never forget
Is Lourdes, the Village of St. Bernadette

Ave, ave, ave Maria
Ave, ave, ave Maria

There, like a dream, this wonderful night
I gazed at the grotto aglow in the light
A feeling divine swept over me there
I fell to my knees as I whispered the prayer

Ave, ave, ave Maria
Ave, ave, ave Maria

Now I am home, I'm happy to be
Telling of places I've travelled to see
One little town I'll never forget
Is Lourdes, the Village of St. Bernadette

Ave, ave, ave Maria
Ave, ave, ave Maria

Eula Parker, 1959

My Grandfather's Clock

My grandfather's clock
Was too large for the shelf,
So it stood ninety years on the floor;
It was taller by half
Than the old man himself,
Though it weighed not a pennyweight more.
It was bought on the morn
Of the day that he was born,
And was always his treasure and pride;

But it stopped short
Never to go again,
When the old man died.

Ninety years without slumbering,
Tick, tock, tick, tock,
His life seconds numbering,
Tick, tock, tick, tock,
It stopped short
Never to go again,
When the old man died.

In watching its pendulum
Swing to and fro,
Many hours had he spent while a boy;
And in childhood and manhood
The clock seemed to know,
And to share both his grief and his joy.
For it struck twenty-four
When he entered at the door,
With a blooming and beautiful bride;

My grandfather said
That of those he could hire,
Not a servant so faithful he found;
For it wasted no time,
And had but one desire,
At the close of each week to be wound.
And it kept in its place,
Not a frown upon its face,
And its hand never hung by its side.

It rang an alarm
In the dead of the night,
An alarm that for years had been dumb;
And we knew that his spirit
Was pluming his flight,
That his hour of departure had come.
Still the clock kept the time,
With a soft and muffled chime,
As we silently stood by his side.
But it stopped short
Never to go again,
When the old man died.

Ninety years without slumbering,
Tick, tock, tick, tock,
His life seconds numbering,
Tick, tock, tick, tock,
It stopped short
Never to go again,
When the old man died.

Henry Clay Work

Poor Wandering One

Poor wand'ring one!
Though thou hast surely strayed,
      Take heart of grace,
      Thy steps retrace,
Poor wand'ring one!

The Pirates of Penzance, operetta. Composer **Arthur Sullivan**, 1879

Both Sides Now

Bows and flows of angel hair and ice cream castles in the air
And feather canyons everywhere, I've looked at clouds that way.
But now they only block the sun, they rain and snow on everyone.
So many things I would have done but clouds got in my way.

I've looked at clouds from both sides now,
From up and down, and still somehow
It's cloud's illusions I recall.
I really don't know clouds at all.

Moons and Junes and ferris wheels, the dizzy dancing way you feel
As every fairy tale comes real; I've looked at love that way.
But now it's just another show. You leave 'em laughing when you go
And if you care, don't let them know, don't give yourself away.

I've looked at love from both sides now,

From give and take, and still somehow
It's love's illusions I recall.
I really don't know love at all.

Tears and fears and feeling proud to say "I love you" right out loud,
Dreams and schemes and circus crowds, I've looked at life that way.
But now old friends are acting strange, they shake their heads, they say
I've changed.
Something's lost but something's gained in living every day.

I've looked at life from both sides now,
From win and lose, and still somehow
It's life's illusions I recall.
I really don't know life at all.

Joni Mitchell

Big Yellow Taxi

They paved paradise
And put up a parking lot
With a pink hotel, a boutique
And a swinging hot SPOT
Don't it always seem to go
That you don't know what you've got
'Til it's gone
They paved paradise
And put up a parking lot

They took all the trees
And put them in a tree museum
And they charged the people
A dollar and a half just to see 'em
Don't it always seem to go,
That you don't know what you've got
'Til it's gone
They paved paradise
And put up a parking lot

Hey farmer, farmer
Put away that DDT now
Give me spots on my apples
But LEAVE me the birds and the bees
Please!
Don't it always seem to go
That you don't know what you've got
'Til its gone
They paved paradise
And put up a parking lot

Late last night
I heard the screen door slam
And a big yellow taxi
Took away my old man
Don't it always seem to go
That you don't know what you've got
'Til it's gone
They paved paradise
And put up a parking lot

I said
Don't it always seem to go
That you don't know what you've got
'Til its gone
They paved paradise
And put up a parking lot

They paved paradise
And put up a parking lot
They paved paradise
And put up a parking lot

Joni Mitchell (1943–), musician, songwriter and painter

—Joni Mitchell was born in Alberta and raised in Saskatoon, Canada.
   She got the idea for the song "Big Yellow Taxi" during a visit to
   Hawaii. She looked out of the hotel window at the spectacular
   Pacific Mountain scenery, and then down to a parking lot. Joni
   wrote about the song in the early 1970s…"Living in Los Angeles,

smoke—choke. L.A. is bad enough but the last straw came when I visited Hawaii for the first time. It was night-time when we got there so I didn't get my first view of the scenery until I got up the next morning. The hotel room was quite high up so in the distance I could see the blue Pacific Ocean. I walked over to the balcony and there was the picture book scenery, palm trees swaying in the breeze and all. Then I looked down and there was this ugly concrete car park in the hotel grounds. I thought "they paved paradise and put up a parking lot" and that's how the song "Big Yellow Taxi" was born." The song's final verse becomes personal, and Joni recounts the departure of a lover.

_____

Only Forever

Do I want to be with you
        as the years come and go?
Only forever
        if you care to know.
Will I grant all your wishes
        and be proud of the task?
Only forever
        if someone should ask.
How long would it take me
        to be near if you beckon?
Off hand I would figure
        less than a second.
Do you think I'll remember
        how you looked when you smile?
Only forever
        that's putting it mild.

Johnny Burke (lyricist) and **James V. Monaco** (music)

—Written for the film *Rhythm On The River* starring Bing Crosby, 1940.

_____

Brother, Can You Spare A Dime?

They used to tell me I was building a dream, and so I followed the
mob.
When there was earth to plow or guns to bear, I was always there, right
on the job.
They used to tell me I was building a dream, with peace and glory
ahead,
Why should I be standing in line, just waiting for bread?

Once I built a railroad, I made it run, I made it race against time.
Once I built a railroad, now it's done. Brother, can you spare a dime?
Once I built a tower, up to the sun, brick and rivet and lime.
Once I built a tower, now it's done. Brother, can you spare a dime?

Once in khaki suits, gee we looked swell,
Full of that Yankee Doodly Dum,
Half a million boots went slogging through Hell,
And I was the kid with the drum!

Say, don't you remember, they called me Al; it was Al all the time.
Why don't you remember, I'm your pal? Buddy, can you spare a dime?

Written by **Jay Gorney** (music) and **E.Y. "Yip" Harburg** (music) in
1931, during the years of the Great Depression

—"Here is a man who had built his faith and hope in this country.
Then came the crash. Now he can't accept the fact that the bubble
has burst. He still believes. He still has faith. He just doesn't
understand what could have happened to make everything go so
wrong." (E.Y. Harburg)

Any Dream Will Do

I closed my eyes, drew back the curtain
To see for certain what I thought I knew
Far, far away, someone was weeping,
But the world was sleeping
Any dream will do.

I wore my coat, with golden lining
Bright colours shining, wonderful and new
And in the east, the dawn was breaking
And the world was waiting,
Any dream will do.

My golden coat flew out of sight.

The colours faded into darkness.

May I return to the beginning.
The light is dimming and the dream is too.
The world and I we are still waiting
Still hesitating,
Any dream will do
Still hesitating,
Any dream will do.

May I return to the beginning
The light is dimming, and the dream is too.
The world and I, we are still waiting
Still hesitating,
Any dream will do
Give me my coloured coat.
My amazing coloured coat.
Give me my coloured coat.

Composer: **Andrew Lloyd Webber**, lyricist: **Tim Rice**. Sung by
Donny Osmond, *Joseph and the Amazing Technicolor Dreamcoat*

Crest of a Wave

We're riding along on the crest of a wave
And the sun is in the sky.
All our eyes on the distant horizon
Look out for passers-by.
We'll do the hailing
When all the ships are round us sailing.
We're riding along on the crest of a wave
And the world is ours.

Ralph Reader (1903-1982).

—Originally a Sea Scout song, it has been sung in every country of the
world where Scouting exists. Memories of Scout camps (**A. Michael
Warrington**).

King of the Road

Trailer for sale or rent
Rooms to let fifty cents.
No phone, no pool, no pets
I ain't got no cigarettes
Ah, but two hours of pushin' broom
Buys an eight by twelve four-bit room
I'm a man of means by no means
King of the road.

Third boxcar, midnight train
Destination Bangor, Maine.
Old worn out clothes and shoes,
I don't pay no union dues,
I smoke old stogies I have found
Short, but not too big around
I'm a man of means by no means
King of the road.

I know every engineer on every train
All of their children, and all of their names

And every handout in every town
And every lock that ain't locked
When no one's around.

I sing,
Trailers for sale or rent
Rooms to let, fifty cents
No phone, no pool, no pets
I ain't got no cigarettes
Ah, but, two hours of pushin' broom
Buys an eight by twelve four-bit room
I'm a man of means by no means
King of the road.

Written and originally performed by **Roger Miller** (1936–1993)

Old Toy Trains

Old toy trains, little toy tracks;
Little boy toys coming from a sack,
Carried by a man dressed in white and red,
Little boy don't you think it's time you were in bed?

Close your eyes,
Listen to the skies,
All is calm, all is well,
Soon you'll hear Kris Kringle and the jingle bells bringing…

Old toy trains, little toy tracks,
Little boy toys coming from a sack,
Carried by a man dressed in white and red
Little boy don't you think it's time you were in bed?

Close your eyes,
Listen to the skies,
All is calm,
All is well,
Soon you'll hear Kris Kringle and his jingle bells bringing…

Old toy trains, little toy tracks,
Little boy toys coming from a sack,
Carried by a man dressed in white and red,
Little boy don't you think it's time you were in bed?

Close your eyes,
Listen to the skies,
All is calm,
All is well,
Soon you'll hear Kris Kringle and the jingle bells bringing ..

Old toy trains, little toy tracks,
Little boy toys coming from a sack,
Carried by a man dressed in white and red,
Little boy don't you think it's time you were in bed?
Little boy don't you think it's time you were in bed?

Written by **Roger Miller**. Later sung and recorded by Nana Mouskouri

---

SPRING BREAK

In 1997, my wife and I decided to take a trip to Arizona. At Vancouver Airport we had a roll-aboard each so no luggage to check in. We boarded our flight, a Boeing 737, WestJet.

Good flight, bumpy at times. We were served a snack of strawberry yoghurt, bagel, cream cheese, box of raisins, coffee, very welcome.

Two-and-a-half-hour flight. An announcement came over the loud speaker system, "We hope you have had a good flight with WestJet. Please fasten your seatbelts in preparation for landing and welcome to Sioux City, Iowa." We all looked at each other in dismay—thinking we must have somehow got on the wrong plane. Then the voice came back, "April first!"

Everyone very pleasant and helpful at the airport. We picked up our car from AVIS, a brand new Dodge Stratus, never heard of it. Four-door, sedan, four cylinder, very nippy.

We got good directions with a map from the lady at the AVIS desk. No trouble getting out of the airport onto 24th Street and finding our Best Western Airport Inn. Basic, not fancy, nice and clean. Two queen size beds, non-smoking. $81.00 US per night.

Next day, April 2nd, we set off for Scottsdale and Tucson. We liked Scottsdale very much. Wide streets, lots of Hispanic influence in the stores. Everyone very pleasant and helpful. Warm and sunny. Free parking everywhere. Huge library, beautiful building. Lots of green grass, pools, fountains and very colourful flowers. Would come back here anytime.

Michael remembered that Maureen O'Sullivan (Tarzan's Jane) was said to be living here in retirement. We hoped we might bump into her but no such luck.

One extraordinary thing—there was a notice on the door of the library: "No Weapons Allowed. To Check Your Weapons, Phone This Number...."

We drove on to Tucson. Countryside very flat, desert like with lots of cactus and low scrub. We saw a huge ostrich farm selling ostrich meat. Arrived in Tucson and booked into motel. Found we were in time for the Manager's Happy Hour, 5:30—7:30 p.m. Two free drinks each and not just beer or wine—amazing. And this is every night apparently.

Next day we set off for Xavier Mission situated on a huge Indian Reservation ½ hour drive away. Large adobe building. The base of which is volcanic rock. Beautiful artistic handpaintings on the side walls, colourful religious depictions. Many statues. Nearby school for American Indian children.

The church has capacity for 100 people. Simple wooden benches. Restoration work still going on. Maintained by American Indians. We visited the interesting museum at the Mission. While we were there we met some English people who said they had been to a place called Lake Havasu—we had never heard of it. They said it was worth a visit.

Lunch at a Chinese Restaurant called China Bay. Three waitresses, all Mexican. We could see some of the cooks—one Chinese, one Black, one Caucasian, one Mexican. The service was like lightning. Food was good. Michael's fortune cookie said, "You would have made a good lawyer." We noticed many, many overweight men and women, young and old. Always seemed to be eating something unsuitable.

Decided to go to Nogales in Mexico. Weather just awful, cold and raining. Paid $4.00 to park this side of the border and then walked across into Mexico. Nogales is just like Tijuana. Very touristy. Kids selling gum, women begging. Men bugging you to take a taxi, every store selling the same things. We went into the first store we came to which was selling leather goods and Helen picked out a leather belt - $14.00 US without bargaining. Very cold and wet. We walked back to the car through driving rain and drove back to the motel in Tucson.

Up early on April 4th and decided to drive to the Grand Canyon via Sedona and Flagstaff. We saw a Cardinal bird on a tree beside the motel. Brilliant red bird about the size of a starling with a lovely song.

Heading towards Sedona, we were surprised to see snow at the side of the road and after a little while it began <u>SNOWING</u>!

We stopped at Sedona, hilly area surrounded by huge red rocks. Obviously a popular holiday area, but today there was snow everywhere and IT IS COLD.

Stayed overnight at Days Inn and breakfast the next day at The Coffee Pot. Very popular, very busy. Huge restaurant with 300 items on the menu! They serve breakfast all day—101 different omelettes!

Weather cold, windy and raining at times. Snow on the ground. Visibility closed in to about 30 yards. We saw several cars and a truck which had slid off the road.

This is Arizona!

We decided to pass up on the Grand Canyon and head west to Lake Havasu. As we headed west, the weather improved, blue skies, white fluffy clouds and sunshine <u>at last</u>.

Arrived at Lake Havasu Saturday, 5th of April, in beautiful warm sunshine.

Next morning we sat on the patio for a while in the sunshine—lovely! The motel was situated on the edge of the lake under London Bridge. Then we went on a 45 minute boat trip for 15 miles around the lake and learned the most interesting history of how Lake Havasu City came to be.

Thirty-three years ago there was nothing here!

Checked into our motel about 4:30 p.m.—in time to change and hurry out to the pool.

Helen enjoyed a 40 lap swim and we sat around the pool in the glorious warm sunshine. Six girls in bikinis came out to enjoy the pool and had a great time—(so did Dad!)

London Bridge was originally constructed in London, England in 1831. By 1962 the bridge was not sufficiently strongly constructed to support the increased load created by modern traffic and it was slowly sinking into the mud. The City of London decided to sell the bridge providing whoever bought it would use it as a working bridge and not just a tourist attraction.

Robert McCulloch was the Chairman of McCulloch Oil Corporation and he decided to buy the bridge. The bridge was carefully disassembled and each piece was numbered and shipped to some vacant land beside the Colorado River, Arizona. Re-assembly began, piece by piece, brick by brick. Twenty-two million pounds of granite (10,276 pieces altogether) and it was completed in late 1971. It was constructed beside the Colorado River which was then diverted under the bridge so that it would then be a working bridge.

The street lamps on the bridge were constructed from Napoleon's cannons, which had been seized and kept in storage. The cannons were melted down and forged into lamps for the bridge. In World War II during the London Blitz, although the bridge never sustained heavy damage, there are still visible indentations by cannon shells fired by the German Fighter Bombers.

Lake Havasu is now a popular tourist destination. Condos that were built for $79,000 originally, now worth $400,000 US in 1997. After four days it was time to head home again but we still remember our pleasant stay in Lake Havasu—we would go back there anytime.

A. Michael Warrington

STRESS

How to Tell Type A From Type B Behaviour

Type A
- Sharp, aggressive style of speech; the end of the sentence is faster.
- Easily bored - tunes out, only pretending to listen.
- Always eats, talks and walks quickly.

- Impatient with people who dawdle. For example, saying, "Yes, yes" to speed up someone else's speech, or worse yet, finishing their sentences for them.
- Polyphasic. For example, eating, shaving and reading all at the same time. (Needs to take care to avoid getting dressed and taking the shower at the same time.)
- Selfish. Interested only in conversation about things that relate to him or her. Tries to steer conversation his or her way, or tunes out. (After spending considerable time talking about himself on a TV talk show, a Type A author turned to the host of the program and said, "Well, enough of all this talk about me. Let's talk about you. Tell me, what did you think about my book?")
- Feels guilty when relaxing.
- Not observant. Can't remember details of rooms and so on. Most likely to be the one to lose keys, sunglasses, pens.
- Aims for things worth having, not things worth being.
- Very challenged by another Type A individual. Sparks can fly. This is particularly bad if two Type A's are married to each other.
- Physical signs: Very assertive, tense, leans forward, shoulder blades seldom touch the chair.
- Believes success comes from doing things faster; thus, keeps up a very fast pace. Believes that when you are skating on thin ice, the only thing you have going for you is speed.
- Measures success mainly by numbers; for example, more interested in the number of goals scored than with the pleasure of playing the game.

Type B

- Not characterised by the above traits.
- Seldom feels any time urgency, but can be just as ambitious.
- Very easy going. Not hostile.
- Plays a game for fun, not just to win.
- Can relax without guilt and work without agitation; in the long run can get just as much work done as a Type A.
- Is often more efficient. For example, a Type A friend of mine was watching an old woodcutter stacking one piece of wood at a time against his garage. My friend became so agitated at the

apparent slow pace that he rushed outside, picked up five logs at once, and with a frenetic expenditure of energy, started his own stack of wood. After 20 minutes, he collapsed, almost exhausted, back aching, with his pile of wood only a fraction as large as the old man's. Type Bs, it seems, often win because of their steadiness and their economy of movement. (Perhaps this is what the old "Hare and Tortoise" fable was trying to tell us.)

Conclusion:

Do not allow Type A behaviour to narrow your coronary arteries, undermining your family life and shortening your time on earth. Pause, reflect and rest on your priorities.

It is just as simple to join the Type B team. You must first recognize that your ambitions, goals, and lifestyle can be better achieved with the Type B personality, and that success does not depend on the frenetic nervous energy of the Type A personality. As a bonus, changing to Type B behaviour will give you strength instead of weakness in your health and probably in the personal quadrants of your life.

From *The Joy of Stress* by **Dr. Peter G. Hanson**

SURPRISE

Dear Ann:

I have been a fan of your column ever since I learned to read. I never thought I would end up writing to you, but like so many others, here I am.

I met a wonderful fellow last year and six months later moved in with him. He is 39 by the way, so what happened came as a complete shock to me.

It was very early in the morning and we were both sound asleep. All of a sudden I felt this strange unfamiliar object sticking me in the ribs. I wondered if I were lying on the remote control or perhaps a set of keys. When I reached the object, I had to hold my breath to keep from screaming and waking him up. It was a top set of dentures.

I managed to stay calm although I have never been so shocked in my life. I placed the choppers near his hand so he could find them easily when he woke up. I then rolled over and tried to go back to sleep but I couldn't get over the fact he had kept such a secret from me.

Soon he woke up and I could hear him feeling around for something. He then got up and went to the bathroom.

It has been six months since I discovered his teeth and I am wondering how long he will remain silent. Should I have told him I found them? Now I feel as if I am the one who is keeping a secret.

I have tried several times to steer the conversation to false teeth and make it easy for him but it is not a subject that comes naturally. I don't want him to think I would love him less or that I would make fun of him.

It does make me wonder, however, if he can keep a secret like THIS how many other secrets does he have?

What should I do?

AT A LOSS IN NEVADA

DEAR NEVADA:

There is nothing you should do or say. The fact that he hasn't told you he has false teeth is not a reflection on his character, his integrity or anything else. This is an intensely personal matter that has nothing to do with you.

In order to get a better perspective, ask yourself if YOU had false teeth would you tell him?

Ann Landers

THE PERFECT GUEST

People often complain about guests and visitors who stay too long. We have never found that to be a problem. Often we wish they could stay longer.

However, there is the problem of a guest who feels obliged to "help." That is, the guest who insists on "helping" in the kitchen.

Some guests manage to do this in a way which is genuinely helpful, such as clearing the table. More help than that can become a problem when a guest helpfully empties the dishwasher and then puts things away so that we can "never find them again."

To my mind the ideal guest, having said, "Can I help?" settles down to read the paper or watch TV following the answer, "That's very kind of you but we can manage. Please sit down and relax; that's what you're here for."

A. Michael Warrington

THE PRAIRIES

I drove through in early August, when the surrounding fields were vast tapestries of purple flax and yellow canola stretching to the edges of a sapphire sky. Sweet-scented breezes riffled across acres of wheat, like waves on a prairie ocean. Marshmallow clouds, the kind drawn by preschoolers, scattered low overhead, their shadows rolling like fast moving ships over the lush farmland. Here and there, faded red barns and weathered sheds—icons of an earlier age when farms were still owned by families—stood like arthritic sentries atop gently rolling fields.

The afternoon sun, God's spotlight, had transformed a pile of precisely stacked hay bales into a golden pyramid.

Julie Ovenell-Carter, writer, in *Driving through the Prairies in August*

THEATRE

We remember not only the failures that might have been avoided, but also the successes already fading in older people's memories. The plays themselves may be in print, but they were written to be seen and heard,

not read. A few aging players, as they wiped the grease paint and cold cream off their faces, recollect the plays' triumphant first appearances. It is all going, going, gone; a lift of the voice, a gesture, a look, that were marvels and things of beauty in their time. So, thinking about the Theatre, I cling to my belief that in its own time, somewhere along the fourth dimension, everything still exists: The lift of the voice, that gesture, that look, they are still there. I know that, when I think about the Theatre I only wonder when at least some part of our minds will be able to travel in time, to recapture the past that has not really vanished at all, to see the old velvet curtains rising and falling again. To applaud once more the brave players.

Margin Released, **J.B. Priestley** (1894–1984) English journalist and playwright

---

THREE WISE WOMEN

Would have…
>Asked directions,
>Arrived on time,
>Helped deliver the baby,
>Cleaned the stable,
>Made a casserole,
>Brought practical gifts and
>There would be peace on Earth.

Source Unknown

TRAVEL

Hey family, made it this far to Anne Worby's and Sarah Horsfall's.
>Flight here was an ordeal; Got on the plane in Vancouver and sat, not moving, for an hour while the baggage handlers handled the

baggage, slo-o-o-o-o-wly onto the plane. Making us one hour late to start off with.

I had requested a window seat and, naturally, got a middle seat between two big, fat ladies who hogged the arm rests; I had to eat my meal with elbows tucked WAY into my waist. There was a restless little boy right behind me who couldn't help kicking my seat the WHOLE trip; it felt like turbulence the entire way (precious little darling).

Touched down in Glasgow to let off a few passengers. It was apparently a typical Scottish summer's day, pelting down with rain. Two numbskulls got off the plane who were not supposed to. So the flight attendants had to count us all by hand, then match our names to the manifest, then trundle a set of stairs up to the plane so that we could all get off and identify our luggage. Two bags that were left over were to be taken away to be "completely destroyed." Slow baggage handlers, plus terrorist alert, equals 3+ hours late and counting.

Arrived at Gatwick terminal less 30 feet; the docking mechanism was malfunctioning so we had to wait for someone with a screwdriver and widget to come and fix it. Baggage handlers plus Scottish terrorists plus technical difficulties equals 4 hours late.

Have a great summer everyone. I'm sure I will, soon. Everyone here (Anne, Sarah, David, Rachel) says hello.

Michael G. Warrington—trip to England, August, 2004

Dining Out Once in Queensland, Australia

We decided to dine at the hotel. At dinner, Allan ordered red snapper.

"You not heard of Ciguatera then?" I said casually.

"Of course I haven't b.... heard of it." He replied through clenched teeth. "What now?"

"It's nothing" I said.

"Of course it must be something or you wouldn't have mentioned it. What is it? Am I sitting in it? Is it on my head? What?"

"No, it's a kind of toxin endemic to tropical waters. It accumulates in certain fish."

"Like red snapper, for instance?"

"Well, especially red snapper actually."

He considered this with a kind of slow, catatonic nod. I think jet lag was kicking in. It can do terrible things to one's equilibrium.

"I'm sure there's nothing to worry about." I added reassuringly. "I mean, if there was an outbreak, snapper wouldn't be on the menu, would it. Unless, of course," I stopped there.

"What?"

"Well, unless you were to be the first case. It has to start with somebody, after all. But, hey, what are the chances of that? One in a hundred? One in twenty?"

"I want you to stop this right now."

"Of course." I agreed at once. "I'm sorry. Do you want to change your order?"

"No."

"The symptoms include, but are not limited to, vomiting, severe muscle weakness, loss of motor control, paresthesia of the lips, general lassitude, myalgia and paradoxical sensory disturbances - that is, feeling hot surfaces as cold and vice versa. Death occurs in about 12 percent of cases."

"I'm telling you to stop it right now."

The waitress came with our drinks. "This snapper" Allan said with forced casualness. "It's all right, is it?"

"Oh, yeah. It's beaut."

"I mean, it hasn't got—what is it, Bryson?"

"Ciguatera."

She gave us a befuddled look. "No, it comes with chips and salad."

We exchanged glances.

"Would I be right in assuming you are not from around here?" I asked.

Her puzzlement deepened. "No, I'm from Tazzie. Why?"

"Just wondered."

I whispered to Allen, "She's from Tasmania."

He leaned towards me and whispered back, "Yes, so?"

"Their snapper are okay."

"Is it possible to change my order, love?"

She stared at him heavily for a moment, the way young people do when they realize they are being asked to take 20 steps they hadn't budgeted for and with a martyred air, went off to find out. A minute later she reported back that permission had been granted to change his order.

Dining Out In Queensland

"Excellent!" said Allen with sudden enthusiasm, perusing the menu anew.

"I'll have the sirloin and chips." he announced. "Medium rare, please."

He turned to me, "No horrid diseases I should know about with regard to beef? Queensland Beef Palsy or anything like that?"

"You should be fine with steak."

"Steak it is then." He handed her the menu. "And easy on the Ciguatera," he called after her. "And keep the beers coming," he added further.

In a Sunburned Country by **Bill Bryson**, 2000

First Trip Back

The big, powerful DC8 Jet slammed and skidded gently down onto the tarmac and continued to hurtle forward before coming to a halt and taxiing to the airport terminal.

We were back in England again. The year was 1967. Nothing could have prepared us for the impact that the sights and sounds of our original homeland would make upon us after ten years of absence. In our hired car we wended our way down the country byways, avoiding the main roads, to the house that we had rented for a month at Emsworth in Hampshire. It was like coming home again. The house was adequately furnished, situated on a quiet road, with a typical English garden consisting of an area of pleasant lawn, apple trees, borders of flowing plants and shrubs. We had completely forgotten the indescribably delicate perfumes wafted by the breeze in an English garden. Later someone was to say to us that South Africa is "a country where the birds don't sing, the flowers have no smell and the women have no morals." Leaving aside the latter part of the quotation, we were now re-living and savouring the unique quality of England in summer. Strolling down a country road, it seemed that even the hedgerows had a beautiful aroma which was all their own.

The next day we set off to visit relatives and on the way we stopped at a pub with a garden and tables and chairs. Memories of times long gone came flooding back as I carried out a tray with a pint of mild and bitter, a shandy and a couple of bags of potato crisps. The smell and taste of the first pint of draft malt and hops was almost indescribable.

We had reserved seats for the summer Passing Out Parade at the Royal Military Academy, Sandhurst. The weather was beautiful. The buildings, both old and new, had never looked better in their setting of vast areas of gently sloping grass, woods and small paved roads. A thousand Cadets were on parade in dress uniform and marching in drill formation to the accompaniment of the Military Band in superb perfection. Field Marshal Montgomery gave the address in his inimitable style and reminded the Officer Cadets that they could never begin to control men until they had first learned to control themselves.

We found ourselves seated among a strata of people that we had completely forgotten even existed. The upper class English accents fell most strangely on our ears. With lively interest we glanced about us at the gold braided high ranking officers seated around with their elegantly turned out wives and daughters, who were evidently enjoying it as much as we were.

At the end of the parade, the Passing Out Troop marched in slow time up the steps of the Academy followed by the Adjutant in time honoured fashion on his white charger. The band played Auld Lang Syne and it was all very nostalgic.

Richard and I took a day off to go to Brands Hatch to see the International Sports Car Race Meeting. With the closely interweaving and winding circuit, we were able to see almost every part of the track without having to move and the shattering roar of the cars as they flashed past us was sufficiently exciting.

We had timed an advertisement to appear in the Daily Telegraph on the morning after our arrival asking for a girl to act as a mother's help. To our astonishment we had 56 replies by letter, telegram and personal call. One of the applicants was an excellent girl who only lived two roads from our house, a most self possessed young lady of 18 who was perfectly at home taking charge of our domestic arrangements, completely unflustered by our normally exuberant seven children. Susan accompanied us on local forays and outings, introducing us to sea bathing perfection at West Wittering. Prior to this we had had our first swim at Southsea and Richard remarked that it was like having a warm bath in comparison with the icy dip we were used to in Victoria, British Columbia. West Wittering was ideal—there was plenty of parking for cars, large areas of grass, masses of flat white sand and clean Channel Sea which was not too cold. The time we spent there was all too short.

We visited a branch of the school my wife had once attended as a boarder in Hampshire. This was a school for girls in 80 acres of beautiful rolling grassland and woods seen at its pastoral best in summer sunshine. It was run by Nuns and I was impressed by their youth and freshness. There were lay teachers as well and on our tour through the school we were pleased to see the light, airy classrooms and up to date Science and Biology labs.

We visited Southsea and Portsmouth. Nelson's Flag Ship at the Battle of Trafalgar, H.M.S. Victory, excellently preserved in dry dock in Portsmouth Harbour—an impressive sight as one walks towards it. It seems to tower over its immediate surroundings and seemed much bigger than I expected or remembered. Made of good English oak and kept in excellent repair and renovation, our children clambered everywhere it was allowed to clamber; the older ones trying to imagine what it must have been like to live and go through battles on this great old ship. There were three long rows of cannon along each side of the ship, one above the other, and we were told that all the guns on one side of the ship could not be fired at the same time or the ship would turn over with the recoil. The entire crew in those days were provided with one hot meal a day, even in the heat of battle if possible, and our Royal Marine guide informed us that "things haven't changed much since."

Into Dorset, along quiet little country roads, past Wool to Bovington Camp, where to the delight of the boys we attended the Royal Armoured Corps Open Day. They climbed in and out of massive tanks, peered down gun barrels, kept well out of the way as the huge, clanking, squealing, roaring beasts crunched by within a few feet and went for a ride in an armoured car. We finally had to drag them away with great difficulty from the Tank Museum, which housed various tanks from World War I as well as Russian, German, British and American tanks from World War II.

With our first month now at an end, we headed towards Berkshire for the second month of our holiday. The Rectory was a lovely old English house in acres of garden with lots of bedrooms, and better still an enormous cupboard filled with toys from top to bottom. The house had a large kitchen with a huge wooden table and a remarkable dishwasher. It must have been one of the first dishwashers ever made. After all the dishes had been loaded, it revolved slowly in a most dignified manner, gently chugging and whirring, for exactly nine and a half minutes, at the end of which time the dishes were all washed. They were then left in the machine to drain dry.

In every house we rented there was a wonderful daily woman employed by the owners and we were very happy to carry on with the arrangement.

Richard went off to stay at his uncle's farm but unfortunately after two days a message came to say that he was ill with a temperature and tummy ache. This turned out to be appendicitis and my first disillusionment came when I took him to the local hospital in Reading. To say that this institution had seen better days would be a kindness. The area inside the entrance was bolstered up with scaffolding. I informed the porter that I had a 10-year-old lad with acute appendicitis and he told me to go down various corridors to the ward, leaving me with the impression that it was entirely up to me how I got him there. So Richard hopped on my back and we set off down and around a number of corridors until we found the ward. On the way we passed some dilapidated looking wheelchairs with stained canvass seats and loose backing. At the ward we were received by a rather strained, preoccupied ward sister and Richard was admitted. His appendix was removed that afternoon. Visiting later, I found him in a small crowded ward immediately next door to a glass cubicle room, in the centre of which stood a baby's crib with a hanger holding gowns to one side. This was obviously an isolation area. The baby in the crib looked critically ill and was cyanosed. I did not think that a patient requiring isolation should be nursed immediately next to an acute surgical ward even though there was a glass window between. In four days Richard was ready to come home and I packed him out of the ward, once more on my back. My first impression of an English hospital was jarring.

We settled in to enjoy the peace and quiet beauty of the surroundings at the Rectory. In the soft light of the early morning it was utterly beautiful to look out of the bedroom window at the tranquillity of the country scene. There were a number of very large trees in the garden and birds would alight gently on their nests among the branches, now and again rising gracefully into the air to flutter and soar to another vantage point. A little later in the day we used to watch the harvesting going on all around us and I remember looking from the house and seeing Michael, oblivious to all else, leaning on the gate at the bottom of the garden watching intensely as the harvester worked his way up and down the fields. I could not help wishing that we could live sufficiently in the country that we could hear and see the harvesting every summer.

The garden was a children's paradise with lots of room for running, climbing and jumping in perfect safety with a long bank down which they delighted to roll and slide completely naked.

During all this time I had been looking at nursing homes for my parents. They were no longer able to look after themselves and were now in a home run by the Council but they were not at all happy there. Their situation made me feel I should do something to try and improve it. However, finding another place proved to be difficult—they were all either miles away in isolated parts or were otherwise unsuitable.

The idea of moving back to England suddenly became quite pressing. We knew why we had left—we felt that we had been forced to leave. Having undertaken three years of hospital posts as part of my own training program for the challenge and variety of general practice followed by one year's trainee assistantship, I found literally two hundred doctors applying for the same openings in general practice as myself. Time after time I was informed by general practice principals that there were two hundred applicants for the post. My wife and I would drive from one end of England to the other, not infrequently finding eleven other doctors sitting around drinking tea and orange juice "short listed" for the post like ourselves. I finally decided this was ridiculous; there were too many doctors chasing too few jobs. I made up my mind to go overseas where doctors were in short supply and there was work to be done. We left for Canada in the fall of 1957. Canada was all that we expected and more—yet now we were thinking of coming back to England.

To our surprise the tables had now been turned completely—practices were going begging and general practice principals were telling me that they did not interview doctors for the vacancies anymore—the doctors interviewed them. In an absolutely delightful town in Sussex, barely ten miles from Horsham, a principal told me that they had given up trying to find a third doctor for their practice. They had "trimmed off the periphery" and had decided to keep it reduced to a two-man practice.

We found ourselves with a harrowing decision to make and felt we should now return, mainly for family reasons. An advertisement in a newspaper brought a quick reply from a lady who was willing to rent her furnished house for a whole year. The house was situated in West

Sussex, in a lovely part of the countryside, on a convenient bus route to the nearest town and close to schools. The only snag was that this house would not be ready for a month after I was due to return to Canada and I was anxious to get the family settled. Another advertisement in the local newspaper produced another furnished house, about a mile from the one we were going to rent for a year, and this would be available for the month we needed.

On our way to West Sussex we saw three jets streaking vertically into the sky, and driving down a secondary road we found ourselves in the midst of one of Britain's air shows. For the rest of the day we regaled ourselves with the spectacle of stunting aircraft, flashing jets and highly skilled and dangerous looking acrobatics, including two young girls who stood on the wings of two aircraft holding on with reins. We saw one of the Battle of Britain's Spitfires and one of the last Lancaster Bombers, said to have taken part in the Dambusting raid, flying around and around the airfield.

We moved into the house in West Sussex. This was a most interesting old house, designated an Ancient Monument, having been rented out to its previous occupant for 3 pounds sterling a week for the past 30 years. Naturally, we were paying more rent than that. The house dated from Tudor times and, as an Ancient Monument, no changes or renovations were allowed to be made to it except those repairs which were absolutely necessary. About two dozen pigeons used to settle on the roof every night, and walking in the garden in the evening darkness, it was wonderfully peaceful to hear their murmuring and cooing.

The house also had two cats and at the back of the garage was a retired race horse. He had once been owned by the Crazy Gang. My daughter is crazy about horses and is a good rider but we could never catch him. One day (great excitement) he somehow got out of the gate and took off—he was brought back much to his disgust.

Behind the house there was a huge hole at the end of the garden with an overhanging tree and a long, thick rope on which the boys used to swing to their hearts' content, usually managing to drop into the mud below. Then they would all troop into the kitchen covered in mud from head to foot and as happy as could be.

The road leading down to this lovely old house was one of the narrowest I have ever seen in my life. We had a Mini and it is no exaggeration to say that the sides of our car brushed the bushes on either side of the road. Past the house this road became part of a country walk, and all around this house there were long walks that one could take for mile after mile.

One day a strange lady appeared at our gate mounted on a magnificent horse, dressed in a magnificent black riding habit with a black bowler hat, holding a riding crop in her hand and sitting most majestically in side saddle fashion. She was intrigued to hear that we had all come from Canada and stood talking with us for quite a long time and kindly agreed to let me take pictures of her on her horse.

Later we were informed that she actually owned the house we were renting and that she also owned the little houses and farms you could see for miles around, as well as a vast estate in Scotland and a large area of land in North Africa.

Our children were now starting in their first English school. We were impressed by the lively, go-ahead Head Master and the layout of this brand new school built by the government. A cooked dinner was provided for the all the children everyday for the sum of 1 shilling and 6 pence each. The Head Master told me that the food was well cooked and they were not allowed to keep any of the food—if any of it is left—"It has to be thrown away the same day."

With the family settled comfortably, I now returned to Canada in the hope and expectation that I would be able to sell my house, find someone to take over my practice and then return to my family to reside again in England.

It was not going to work out quite like that.

A. Michael Warrington

TRIBUTE

Like the sun, she bathed us in her warm glow. Now that the sun has set and the cool of the evening has come, some of the warmth we absorbed is flowing back toward her.

Archbishop of Canterbury, **George Carey**

—At the Queen Mother's funeral, Westminster Abbey, April 9, 2002

ULYSSES

The little boy named Ulysses Macauley one day stood over the new gopher hole in the backyard of his house on Santa Clara Avenue in Ithaca, California. The gopher of this hole pushed up fresh, moist dirt and peeked out at the boy, who was certainly a stranger but perhaps not an enemy. Before this miracle had been fully enjoyed by the boy, one of the birds of Ithaca flew into the old walnut tree in the backyard and after settling itself on a branch, broke into rapture, moving the boy's fascination from the earth to the tree. Next, best of all, a freight train puffed and roared far away. The boy listened, and felt the earth beneath him tremble with the moving of the train. Then he broke into a run, swifter than any life in the world.

When he reached the crossing, he was just in time to see the passing of the whole train, from locomotive to caboose. He waved to the engineer, but the engineer did not wave back to him. He waved to five others who were with the train, but not one of them waved back. They might have done so, but they didn't. At last a Negro appeared, leaning over the side of the gondola. Above the clatter of the train, Ulysses heard the man singing:

"Weep no more my lady, oh weep no more today.
We will sing one song for the old Kentucky home.
For the old Kentucky home far away."

Ulysses waved to the Negro too, and then a wondrous and unexpected thing happened, this man, black and different from all the others, waved back to Ulysses, shouting: "Going home, boy,—going back where I belong!"

The small boy and the Negro waved to one another until the train was almost out of sight.

Then Ulysses looked around, there it was, all around him, funny and lonely—the world of his life. The strange weed-infested, junky, wonderful, senseless yet beautiful world. Walking down the track came an old man with a rolled bundle on his back. Ulysses waved to this man too, but the man was too old and too tired to be pleased with a small boy's friendliness. The old man glanced at Ulysses as if both he and the boy were already dead.

The little boy turned slowly and started for home. As he moved, he still listened to the passing of the train, the singing of the Negro and the joyous words: "Going home, boy—going back where I belong!" He stopped to think of all this, loitering beside a China-ball tree and kicking at the yellow, smelly, fallen fruit of it. After a moment, he smiled the smile of the Macauley people—the gentle, wise, secret smile which said "Hello" to all things.

When he turned the corner and saw the Macauley home, Ulysses began to skip, kicking up a heel. He tripped and fell because of this merriment, but got to his feet and went on.

His mother was in the yard, throwing feed to the chickens. She watched the boy trip and fall and get up and skip again. He came quickly and quietly and stood beside her, then went to the hen nest to look for eggs. He found one. He looked at it a moment, picked it up, brought it to his mother and very carefully handed it to her, by which he meant what no man can guess and no child can remember to tell.

The Human Comedy, **William Saroyan** (1908–1981), American author

---

VACUUM CLEANER SALESMAN

Mike's First Job

Mike had a few months to gain some work experience just after graduating from high school. He applied for a job selling vacuum cleaners: $10.00 an hour sounded pretty good at the time. He had to attend a motivational talk along with a few other potential vacuum cleaner salespeople.

The man giving the talk was a sharply dressed chap with argyle socks. He delivered a pep talk and after telling each vacuum cleaner salesperson where to go on their rounds, his final exhortation was "Sell! Sell! Sell!." Each salesman had to provide his own car and he learned that the $10.00 an hour only applied when you actually arrived at the place where you were supposed to sell the vacuum cleaner. It did not include travelling time. Mike soon found that hauling a heavy vacuum cleaner out of an elevator in an apartment building in long endless corridors with swing doors while you held the door open with your foot and hauled the vacuum cleaner though was a bit of a challenge.

On calling on the first potential client, he found that the sole occupant of the apartment, which was extremely small, did not have any carpets and he unfortunately only had one arm. On assembling the vacuum himself, Mike had to struggle to attach the attachment. It did not seem likely that the poor handicapped fellow would be able to affix the attachment with his handicap.

Mike phoned back to head office.

"I can't demonstrate this one."

"Why not?"

Mike did not like to say—well, he's only got one arm—with the man sitting there listening.

Head office kept pressing Mike to explain. Embarrassing.

Michael G Warrington

THE VILLAGE THAT TIME FORGOT

Dorset, England.

It was late in 1943 and life in Tyneham was much the same as usual. The people were going about their usual routines—tending the sheep on the nearby hills, labouring on the farm, running the village shop or working at Tyneham House, which provided much of the material welfare for the community. The villagers had made sacrifices of course, just like the rest of war-torn Britain, but the hamlet nestled in a valley on a pristine stretch of the English south coast remained relatively untouched by the conflict raging across the English Channel.

But this day was different. Talk in the post office was sombre. Mr. Bond, owner of Tyneham House, and much of the surrounding lands had received a telegram: his son was "missing in action." And if that wasn't enough, in the very same post was a letter from the War Office. There was to be a compulsory evacuation of the village "within 28 days and for the duration of the emergency." The shock was tainted with irony. Everyone had feared the arrival of Hitler's Army whose

shadow stretched across continental Europe. Now it was to be the British Army that would occupy Tyneham. However, sacrifices had to be made for the war effort—and besides they could all return when the war was over. So the villagers hurriedly packed their personal belongings and vacated their homes. As the last inhabitants left the village on December 19, 1943, a poignant letter was pinned to the church door:

> "Please treat the Church and houses with care. We have given up our homes, where many of us have lived for generations, to help win the war to keep men free. We shall return one day and thank you for treating the village kindly."

An Elizabethan manor house, a collection of stone cottages, a church and a school, all cradled between towering hills, wide expansive grass land and the blue sea beyond, were left empty among the trees. But the peace of the valley was soon shattered by the noise of vehicles, exploding shells and gunfire from Army exercises.

Within six months Allied troops landed on the beaches of Normandy. A year later Hitler had committed suicide in his Berlin bunker. Europe was free. Across Britain, towns and cities picked up the pieces after heavy bombing and destruction but Tyneham remained off-limits in the hands of the Government and none of the villagers were allowed to return. In the decades that followed, the delightful hamlet succumbed to the ravages of nature and time, crumbling behind barbed wire to become a 20th century ghost village.

Hikers on the delightful Purbeck coastal path can today make an easy detour to Tyneham and explore the remains of the village. From the church, which first had a Rector in 1304, walk along Post Office Row—the main street of the village—and into the shells of the small buildings: The school teacher's house, the labourer's cottage, the shepherd's cottage and the post office which doubled as the general store. More remains of cottages are scattered throughout the village, most inhabited by farm labourers or employees of Tyneham House.

The most interesting building of the hamlet is the restored school room. Exercise books on the desks and named coat pegs are vivid reminders of a lost village life. The attendance register, kept by Miss Woodman, Head Mistress for 14 years from 1908, allows glimpses of a by-gone rural age. In July 1909, she notes:

"The children are being kept away while the mothers carry food to the hayfields."

Another entry in September 1913 reads:

"The attendance is again lower by the absence of Ernest Jewer who has not been to school since the holiday owing to having no boots."

These are all echoes of a very different time, far removed from 21st century life.

The Ministry of Defence has helped to preserve a stunning stretch of coastline, including the 3,000 acres of Tyneham Parish and beyond, home to Peregrine Falcons and other rare species of birds—and so cruelly denying the villagers their homes and community, it may be that their parting wish has been unexpectedly granted. Without the intrusion and demands of modern life, perhaps the village has been treated kindly after all, left to grow old in a beautiful and unspoiled valley. Certainly the village, the archaeology and way of life would not have exerted such interest had the Army not evacuated it almost a lifetime ago.

From *The Village That Died For England* by **Patrick Wright**

A VISIT TO CAMBRIDGE

When the rehearsal ends at six, the chapel doors open to the public for the candlelight evensong service. Choirs have sung services here since 1379. At 6:15, the gowned choristers file in. They sing William Byrd's, "Vigilate" or "Be Ye Watchful." The stone Saints and Prophets lining the east end of the chapel seemed to be listening.

When choristers like my father return after 40 or 50 years—and they frequently do—they find an institution almost indistinguishable from the one they left.

On our trip, my Dad pointed out other things that had changed little since his time here: The well worn stairs he ran up when late for practise; the exquisite blue-red stained-glass window….he showed me the Great Hall where the huge fireplace is set ablaze during Advent in anticipation of the singing of the familiar "Boar's Head Carol."

Later, in the gloom of the empty chapel, Dad put his head back and sweetly sang a line from Handel's "Messiah." He found his return "a solemn experience" he told me. "You realize that you are part of a continuum and that is at once reassuring and extremely humbling."

It was my father's birthday when we attended Choral Evensong at Magdalen College, where he had once been a student. Side by side, we listened as the choir began Palestira's "*Sicut cervus.*" As the music settled on us, gentle as the misty rain outside, I felt unutterable joy. I began to cry, recalling the words I had heard sung so many times on this trip: "As it was in the beginning, it ever, and ever shall be."

Julie Ovenell-Carter, *Globe and Mail*, May 29, 1999

WAGON WHEELS AND PRAIRIE OYSTERS

In 1957 we left England in a state of disillusionment after looking for an opening in general practice for about a year. At one practice we were short listed with eleven others and when we went for our interview, I didn't like the practice anyway.

There was a surplus of doctors in England at that time. The doctors who had been in the services during the War had come back and the people who had studied Medicine during the War went into practice. When those of us who had studied Medicine after the War started looking, there were very few openings left. When I phoned one advertised vacancy, the Principal informed me that he had 200 other applicants for this position but, "As you have taken the trouble to phone me," he said, "I will put you on our short list." We drove 100 miles across England and this is where we found eleven other doctors and their wives sitting in the garden sipping orange juice waiting to be interviewed.

I said to Helen, "This is ridiculous. Let's go where we're needed." So, we applied to come to Canada. In those days, with a British Medical Degree you could practice in the Prairies and the Maritime provinces but not British Columbia or Quebec as these were considered "desirable" places to practice and they already had enough doctors whereas the Prairies and the Maritimes were short of doctors.

So we responded to an advertisement in the *British Medical Journal* and arrived in a small town about 200 miles north of Saskatoon on November 1, 1957 with our son, Richard, who was just three months old. There was heavy snow everywhere and it was 30 degrees below zero.

I was one of two doctors and the other chap had done some surgery. His favourite pastime was opening people up while I gave anaesthetics. My experience of anaesthesia was very limited but I soon became adept at administering an anaesthetic by open ether. It was not very long before I became disillusioned, however, with my associate. He operated on one young man for appendicitis and did not realize until he was "in there" that the young man had already previously had his appendix removed. Wrong diagnosis. He operated on a young girl's neck because she had "a bulge." He thought it was a cyst but a subsequent x-ray showed a hemi-vertebra which had caused the bulge on one side of her neck.

I really did not want to stay there and as we alternated weekends to be on call, I used my free weekends to explore the Province looking for somewhere else to practice.

Saskatchewan is a vast province. Bigger than France, Belgium and Holland combined, though the population of Saskatchewan is less than the city of Birmingham in England.

The roads are all on the grid system, based on square miles. One section is one square mile and the farms vary between one and four sections. There are widely scattered villages and small settlements, some towns and cities. A city in Saskatchewan is considered to be 1,000 people. We were able to find another small town which needed a doctor where I had my own practice, 3,000 patients over 500 square miles, also about 200 miles north of Saskatoon. The "town" itself had no main water, no main drainage, electricity had only gone in the year before we arrived. One might call this a bit of a "culture shock."

Sometimes there was a water shortage, depending on how heavy the snowfall was in the winter. As we had no running water, Helen used to walk into the village to the pump and fill two pails of water and walk back to the house, by which time there would be a layer of ice on top of the pail. On one occasion we were so short of water in the hospital, we had to scrub up using boiled melted snow.

We had a cistern under the house in what would normally have been a basement. This could be filled with water which was used for washing only—not drinking water. A man came around hauling a huge tank of water which he supplied to the houses charging $5.00 for 100 gallons. This could be pumped up to the bathroom for washing only.

We acquired fur hats, warm overcoats, big overboots and warm gloves. The cars had engine block heaters connected to the electrical supply so that the car would start up in the mornings. Cars also had plastic rectangles fitted to the inside of the windows which never iced up. Without them, it would not be possible to see through the windows during the winter.

When the car was parked overnight outside, the bottom of the tire would freeze solid and when you started up the car to drive along it was like driving on square wheels for a while until they thawed out. During one of our drives around Saskatchewan, we met up with a doctor who had trained at the Middlesex Hospital in London where I had trained. During our visit he showed us his outside conservatory where he had half a cow carcass hanging up. This kept it perfectly refrigerated and frozen and he told us that when he needed a steak, he would come out into the conservatory and hack off a piece of meat.

If a car broke down in a blizzard with no help nearby, it could be a hazardous situation. While we were in Saskatchewan a Mountie got stuck in his car in a blizzard and the next day he was found frozen to death.

One of our neighbours said the best way to keep your supply of bread was to "Stick it in the snow, see?"

The town where we practiced had an excellent hospital, small, but well-equipped. It had an x-ray department, an operating room, a laboratory for routine blood work and the staff consisted of a Matron and two part-time Registered Nurses. Also a lab tech who did blood tests and operated the x-ray machine. The hospital had 14 beds and six bassinets for infants.

On the occasions when we were able to get away for a half day to North Battleford, 90 miles to the east, coming home at night across the dark prairie, you could see little twinkling lights in the distance, rather like returning across the sea to a little island.

After a winter blizzard there might be snow drifts almost to the top of the telephone poles. When the blizzard was gone everything was beautifully quiet and still. Blue skies from horizon to horizon and sound travelled a long way. In the early days, folks in isolated farmhouses could hear the jingling of the horse's harness for a long time before father arrived back from the nearest town. At night the skies would be beautifully clear and we could see a phenomenon that we had never seen before, namely the Northern Lights, or *Aurora Borealis*, a beautiful sight in the Northern Hemisphere caused by electrically charged particles entering the Earth's atmosphere, attracted by the Earth's magnetic field.

In the Spring, water from the snow sinks into the earth and for a week or so the gravel roads are covered with slush. The summers are short and very hot. Grass turns brown after about three weeks and there are not many flowers.

The farmers plant their wheat in the Spring and by August, there are thousands of acres of golden wheat waving gently in the breeze underneath brilliant blue skies. There is not a sound to be heard—just earth and sky. You can see a car coming in the distance by a plume of dust. The isolation is complete. The sunsets are gorgeous. It has been well said that the prairies have their own beauty.

I had heard the term Prairie Oyster while in the Army in England. After a heavy night in the Mess someone could ask for a "pick me up" the next day and this was known as a Prairie Oyster. It consisted of one raw egg in Worchester Sauce with vinegar, salt and pepper swallowed in one gulp. On enquiry I was later informed that the term Prairie Oyster on the Canadian Prairies refers to a dish in which the testicles of a young bull (or in some circles a young ram) are cooked, usually fried, and eaten. The name is understood to be a parody of the original dish, intended to make a vile drink sound even more vile. It became known as an effective hangover cure.

In the small town where we were now located (Neilburg, Pop. 200) I was expected to do rather more surgery than I was accustomed to, though I had done some surgery in England. I went down to Chicago to the Cook County General Hospital where I took a course in Practical Surgery. This gave me the confidence to do appendix operations, tonsils when necessary, hernia repairs on the farmers, which were not that uncommon because they were constantly lifting heavy bales. I had done enough Orthopaedics in England to know how to reduce and cast simple uncomplicated fractures. I had done

Obstetrics and Gynaecology in England and was able to do forceps deliveries when the mother was unable to deliver the baby herself.

If a patient was seriously ill they had to be taken to Saskatoon some 200 miles away. This could be difficult in a blowing blizzard. A train came to the village eight miles away but not every day. In the summertime a plane could be brought in from Saskatoon to evacuate a patient. The first time I phoned for the plane, the pilot came on the line and asked me where he could land. I thought if the pilot had done it before he would know where to land but he was new to the situation. The pilot asked me to go and find a good field, find out which way the wind was blowing and phone him back with the details.

There was no one around to ask so I went out in the car and drove a little way out of town and found what looked like a good level field. I wet my finger and held it up to the breeze to determine which way the wind was blowing.

On returning to the hospital, I phoned the pilot again and told him exactly where the field was—I don't remember the details now— say, one mile north and half a mile west with the wind blowing from the west. Someone heard where the plane was going to land and they said, "You can't bring a plane in there—it's a new crop." Well, it just looked like green grass to me and by that time it was too late anyway— the plane was already on the way. Nevertheless, it seemed half the town turned out to watch the plane come in, new crop or no new crop.

For operations, I could call on another G.P. in a village some 25 miles to the north to give a general anaesthetic. When he was unavailable, I had to rely on the Matron. After inducing the patient with intravenous Pentothal, the Matron was sufficiently experienced to keep the patient asleep using ether dripped onto a gauze mask.

On one occasion, I heard a "thump" and when I looked around I found the "anaesthetist" had disappeared. She had passed out momentarily. It was a hot day and the ether fumes had got to her. She bounced up quite quickly and I said, "Are you alright?"

She replied, "Yes, I'm alright." I thought I should close up and postpone the operation. She said, "No, no, I'm fine." So we carried on uneventfully.

Thank goodness nothing ever went wrong. It was the sort of community where the farmers would come in from their outlying farms on a Saturday for their shopping. There was one movie a week on a Saturday night in the local hall. After the movie they would sometimes come to the doctor's house and bang on the door. I would go to the door in my pyjamas and dressing gown and the farmer would say "Doc, Doc, I would like you to listen to my chest before I go back to the farm."

Late one night a man arrived at the hospital with his wife who had a raging toothache. She had a carious lower molar. The nearest dentist was in Lloydminster, some 50 miles away. Under the circumstances extraction seemed the best solution. I did a mandibular block and using the dental forceps that we had the in the hospital I attempted to extract the molar. Lower molars are more difficult to extract than upper molars. This proved to be exceedingly difficult. It would not budge. To get a better grip on the tooth I asked the patient and her husband if they would mind if I could hold her head under my arm, rather like a football, to give a better purchase while trying to pull the tooth. I rocked and tugged as hard as I could but it simply would not budge. I said I was very sorry but I would have to give her a lot of painkillers and she would have to see the dentist in Lloydminster the next day.

This brings to mind a story by our Professor of Anatomy at the hospital in London where I trained. While working as a Casualty Officer, he'd had a patient come in with a severe toothache, so the professor decided to extract it. He was a big man but found he was totally unable to extract the tooth, so he had to send the patient away with some painkillers until the patient could see a dentist.

When he went back to his desk, he found a note left there by the Sister. The note read, "Not failure, low aim is crime."

He determined that this would never happen again and he went to the London Dental Hospital to learn how to extract molars and he became experienced in the art. Years later he worked as a Missionary doctor in China. He used to go around to the villages in his car attending to people who needed the services of a doctor. In one village they did not want to have anything to do with him though he still continued to visit the village on his rounds. Nobody ever wanted to see him.

One day he stopped at this village and got out of his car, took some dental forceps out of his bag, waived it in the air and said, "Has anyone here got a toothache?"

After a little while they brought someone forward who indeed had a bad toothache and a carious tooth, also a bottom molar. However, he extracted it with little fuss or formality, relieving the patient of his tooth and his pain. From that time onward he could do no wrong and they always welcomed him into that village.

While we were in Saskatchewan we heard about the Barr Colonists. The Barr Colony grew out of a scheme originated by an Anglican Clergyman, the Reverend Issac Barr. The Reverend Issac Barr was born in 1847 in Ontario. He became an Anglican Priest and served mainly in Western Canada and the United States. He conceived the notion that he would encourage immigrants to come to the Western Prairies of Canada. He convinced the Canadian Department of the Interior to set aside a huge tract of land north of Saskatoon for British settlers along the Saskatchewan-Alberta border in 1903.

The Reverend Barr placed advertisements in England saying that a veritable promised land awaited settlers in Canada. Each colonist would be given free land, according to the pamphlets. Hundreds of families responded to the advertising, with promised grandiose promises of all kinds of assistance. "Canada needs you. Free farms of 160 acres open for settlement."

Getting to the promised land in the Spring of 1903 was nothing short of disaster. Very few of them were farmers, mostly they were town dwellers, shopkeepers and clerical workers.

After a rough ocean voyage in a ship equipped to handle only about 550 passengers, instead of 1,900, the exhausted immigrants arrived in St. John, New Brunswick where they faced numerous delays and baggage inspections. Eventually they boarded three immigrant trains, none of them with overnight accommodation for the five day trip to Saskatoon.

There they experienced further disillusionment. Army surplus bell tents had been erected to house them and since there was no stationhouse, their luggage was dumped on the prairie. Local merchants charged inflated prices for basic necessities. Far from being provided with transportation, the settlers were expected to buy their own oxen and carts for their belongings.

The colonists had no experience driving oxen and wagons; for some this was too much and they turned back. The rest began homesteading around Lloydminster, named after the Reverend Lloyd, the Chaplain to the group. The first year must have been terrible. Some froze to death. Food was in short supply and they had no proper winter clothing.

"They arrived with tennis rackets."

They lived in tents, wagons and crude sod shacks. When it rained, the rain water dripped through the sod roof into their tea cups.

There is a letter on record from the Reverend Barr to a resident of Belfast, Ireland in 1903.

> "I am in receipt of your letter. The more capital a man has the better, but as you have been in Florida and had experience there, I should judge that any man who can successfully farm in Florida can successfully do so in my colony."

In spite of the hardships, the majority struggled through—a mixture of British stubbornness and insufficient funds to return to the Old Country.

The remaining Colonists became thoroughly frustrated with Barr and accused him of misleading them about conditions on the Prairies. They voted in a new leader, the Reverend Lloyd, and named their first settlement after him (Lloydminster).

Through hard work and sheer perseverance, the settlement survived and eventually began to prosper.

Barr was publicly pelted with rotten eggs and returned to the United States where he worked in various secular jobs before moving to Australia where he died in 1936.

At the time of the early colonization by the Barr Settlers, in those days in the spring, the prairie would look white from buffalo bones which were everywhere. People could get $5 to $6 for a wagon load of buffalo bones and they would be shipped east if they could be got to the nearest railhead.

There used to be millions of buffalo that took all day to pass a camp. What happened to them and where did they all go? By 1900 they were all gone. Nothing left but the bones and buffalo chips (buffalo droppings) which they used for making fires.

Some of the people who lived around Neilburg were descendants of the original Barr Settlers.

The doctor's house was right next to the hospital, which of course was very convenient.

I tried to take a half day one day a week to go to North Battleford for a change of scenery and some shopping.

On more than one occasion we were chased by a truck coming after us at speed, overtaking and pulling up in front of us. "Doc, you've got to come back. I've got a sick man in the back of the truck."

Once I persuaded a lady doctor who was semi-retired, living in North Battleford, married to a bush pilot, to take my place while I went on a holiday for two weeks. We drove to Victoria, BC where the grass was still green and all the flowers were out and Helen said, "Tell you what—I'll stay here with the kids and you go back to Saskatchewan and join us when you can." She doesn't really like me to say this—but it seemed funny at the time—and still does.

I had once read in a geography book at school that Victoria had a Mediterranean climate: a warm, dry summer and a mild, wet winter.

From that time on, I resolved to take the Canadian final exams and try to move to Victoria if at all possible.

When we returned to Neilburg the lady doctor said, "I would not come here again for any amount of money." In those days, before the Pill, the farmer's wives, bless them, seemed to be always pregnant and with 3,000 patients altogether we were often up at a night delivering babies. Although, as Helen would say, "You were not delivering them—the mothers delivered them." Granted. But sometimes the mother needs help and there is an art in helping the mother to deliver without a tear, sometimes having to do a forceps delivery using a pudendal block anaesthetic.

Sometimes farmers would come into town on a Saturday, have too much to drink and roll their cars off the gravel road onto the soft shoulder, then be brought into the hospital with various injuries and broken bones.

The local coroner was located in a town to the east. One time he asked me to carry out a post mortem on a woman who had died in a road accident, to try and determine a cause of death other than from the accident itself! This was carried out in the Sluice Room in the hospital.

A. Michael Warrington

WAR

<u>Meeting Rommel</u>

I was blindfolded and driven off for interrogation. I knew that if the Germans discovered I was Hungarian I would be shot so I put on a Welsh accent and somehow got away with it.

The car stopped. They took off my blindfold and I saw a lovely castle with a river in the distance. Then they pushed me inside.

I was taken before an elegantly dressed officer. He said to me in perfect English, "You're going to meet someone very important. I hope that you will behave with the utmost decency."

I said: "I always behave with the utmost decency, I am a British officer."

I was taken into a beautiful library. At the far end was a desk, behind which a man was sitting. I remembered being told that you should always make someone move towards you if you want to unnerve them. I said to myself: "I'm not bloody well going to be unnerved myself," so I stayed where I was.

To my surprise, the man stood up and started walking towards me. When he was a few feet away, I realized it was Rommel. He asked me to sit and said, through an interpreter, "You're in a very difficult position. My people seem to think you are a saboteur."

Still putting on my Welsh accent, I replied, "If Field Marshall Rommel really thought I was a saboteur, he wouldn't have invited me here."

Rommel said, "So you think this is an invitation, do you?"

"Indeed I do, sir," I replied. "And I am greatly honoured."

Then he began to laugh. So did everyone else and the atmosphere became friendly. Rommel said: "How is my friend, Montgomery?"

I replied, "Unfortunately, I don't know him personally, but I read in the English papers that he is planning an invasion, so you will probably be seeing him soon."

Rommel laughed again, and then he said something unbelievable, "It is a great pity the British and Germans don't get together and fight the real enemy—Russia."

I said, "That's a very interesting idea, but I don't think it would be possible because we don't approve of some of the things that you do."

"What sort of things?" he wanted to know.

"Well, the way you treat the Jews."

"Oh, that is political," he said. "I don't want to know anything about politics, I am a soldier."

I asked Rommel how he thought the French felt about being occupied. He said that the French were perfectly relaxed about it because they had plenty to eat and drink. "If you travel through France you can see just how happy they are," he told me.

I said, "There's nothing I'd like more, but every time I travel with your boys, they blindfold me."

He turned to his A.D.C. and asked, "Is this really necessary?"

And the A.D.C. replied, "Most certainly it is. These saboteurs are very dangerous."

I was sent off to prison. I was not tortured, and a few days later I was sent to a P.O.W. camp. I wondered why my treatment had been so lenient.

A few days later, chatting to a guard, I had my answer. "Of course you wouldn't be here if it wasn't for Field Marshall Rommel," he told me.

I think Rommel did save my life. I have no direct proof apart from that, but I have always thought that he did.

George Lane (1915-2010)

—A Hungarian who moved to England in 1935, Mr. Lane spied for the Special Operations Executive before taking charge of recruitment for Churchill's most elite spy cadre—an organization known only as "X." Two weeks before D-Day he was captured while spying on German coastal defences, which Rommel oversaw.

Rorke's Drift

Seeing thousands of Zulus beating their shields, waving their *assegais* and bearing down on them, one of the solders turned to the Sergeant and said, "Why us?"

And the Sergeant replied, "Because there's no one else, lad."

—This refers to an item of conjectured dialogue between a soldier and a sergeant at the famous battle, Rorke's Drift, which was the successful defence of the Mission Station at Rorke's Drift in Natal Province, South Africa by about 150 British soldiers against 4,500 Zulu warriors. (Zulu Wars, 1879). Eleven Victoria Crosses were awarded to the defenders.

We were taught "unarmed combat" by a huge hulk of an instructor. He showed us how to gouge out a man's eyes, tear off his ears, emasculate him and other endearments.

At the end of the demonstration, the instructor roared at the somewhat weedy Tommy Buxton: "Now then, do you think you could kill a German with your bare hands?"

"Eventually, Sergeant."

Kenneth Rose writing in the *Sunday Telegraph* about Sir Thomas Buxton

----

Pale Ebenezer thought it wrong to fight.
But Roaring Bill (who killed him) thought it right.

Hilaire Belloc (1870 - 1953), French-born English writer

—A message which World War II conscientious objectors might have been called upon to ponder.

Christmas in Amsterdam 1944

Our country had been occupied for four and a half years. The situation had become unbearable since the ill-fated Allied parachute landings in Arnhem, when for a few days we lived in hope of liberation.

The Dutch countryside lay bleak and frozen. Hunger and fear ruled our lives. My father and two brothers were in hiding. But, as Christmas drew near, our hearts were filled with hope.

My mother went ahead with great plans to make this Christmas morning a wonderful event in spite of rationing, the curfew and the problem of getting the three men out of hiding.

There was no tree, but we had some holly branches to decorate the one room and we were able to heat with a tiny little stove, much like an old fashioned top hat.

We even managed to ration our rations, so we could give father and the boys some extra slices of bread and an egg each.

But mother's biggest surprise was to be a half pound tin of butter, real butter, which she had somehow managed to save all those years. She tied it with red ribbon and put it in the centre of the decorated breakfast table.

No candles, but our light was an ingeniously rigged up treadle sewing machine with a bicycle lamp suspended from the antique chandelier. I would sit at the machine and pedal and the whole table would be bathed in light.

The big day came at last—bitter, bitter cold. And, as soon as curfew was lifted, mother and I went to Church. Father and the boys did not risk going to Church as the Gestapo was hot on their tail. But, one by one, they came in through the garden gate and we heard their familiar whistle.

We gathered around the table, thrilled at the sight of a full bread basket and miracle of miracles ... a tin of butter and syrup made from boiled down sugar beets.

While we sang the old familiar carols, mother opened the tin, then ... horrors! We all smelled it at the same time. The butter was completely rancid and inedible.

Mother went into shock with disappointment. Her big surprise ruined. She was inconsolable. It was the most dramatic and sad moment of my life as a child. We all rushed around mother and told her it was just as well, we probably could not have tolerated the butter. We still had the syrup, the eggs and - biggest, unexpected surprise of all—a beautiful bottle of burgundy wine, produced by father out of his secret store.

So there we were, crying, laughing, clinking glasses, forgetting the spoiled butter and eating and drinking to our hearts content.

Then father read to us in English from Dickens *Pickwick Papers* and we all basked in the glow of his voice, the beauty of that tale, and the happiness of our reunion on (as it turned out to be) that last Christmas Day of the war.

Marguerite Gildersleeve (Cousin of Nurse Mieke Steins Bisschop), Heike near Nuland, Holland, 1944

The tank is our weapon, our home and our grave.

Captain Julien Brunet, a French tank captain

MacRobert's Reply

I saw her when Fate struck the blow.
The mother's tears, and head bowed low.
I proudly saw her change mien,
As, valiant as her sons had been,
She rose and cried, "My boys have gone—
They gave their all—The fight goes on.
That's my Reply."

"A mighty plane—our name still flies, no, not in vain your sacrifice.
Such flower of youth like you, but fall
To rise triumphant to the Call.
Yes, such as you St. Michael needs.
Victory is won by valiant deeds.
High in the sky."

"Though no more sons have I to give,
I still can strike—their Spirits live.
The message echoes through the world.
Wherever freemen have unfurled
The flag we love."

"For mothers, children, sweethearts, wives
Who carry on—men give their lives.
For Peace and Freedom—Victory's end.
Fight on, and labour, give and lend.
They watch above."

William Heughan, September 24, 1941

—Dedicated to Lady MacRobert of Douneside who had three sons. Alasdair was killed in a flying accident in 1938 shortly before the outbreak of World War II. Roderic died in a Hurricane in May, 1941 during a strafing attack. Iain died on June 30, 1941 in a Bristol Blenheim over the North Sea. Lady MacRobert's fighting response is history. She donated a Stirling Bomber named MacRobert's Reply and she also donated four Hurricanes to the Royal Air Force.

War Stories

I was in the Headquarters of 3 British Infantry Division, carrying out reconnaissance and contact duties. We were the other side of the River Orne, in an area that had been fought over ever since the drop by 6 Airborne Division. A young Major from one of the forward companies was leading and his orderly was behind and to my left. The explosion was deafening, but I don't remember falling.

After the ear-splitting crash and the blinding light, all seemed very quiet. The Major had dropped on one knee and seemed to be shouting, but I did not hear what he said. The orderly was slumped on the ground and looked all right but had blood on his face. A mist drifted away—momentarily I could see my wife and children sitting in a garden and I called out, but they did not hear me. Now I looked down. My right foot had been blown off and I was gripping my thigh in an attempt to stop the blood flowing. There was no sense of pain.

Much of the tent where I later found myself in bed, was below ground, and one of the M.O.s was speaking to me. Evidently a lot of my remaining leg had been blown away and it would have to be amputated to save what was left—he seemed to be asking my permission and I thought it was very nice of him to put it that way.

I knew that I was very lucky to be alive. Judging by the bits of metal casing dug out of me, the mine that I had stepped on should have killed me instantly. Lucky, too, that I had been picked up so quickly.

Lt.-Col. G.A. Shepperd, Manchester Regiment

227

The Tank

Throughout the tank's history, the most important element of tank warfare has been the tank crewmen—the driver, co-driver, gunner/loader and tank commander, who together make up this close-knit team of professionals.

As one tank crewman wrote in 1945: "We have come to know our colleagues more intimately than a man knows his own brother. We have worked with them, played with them, fought with them, eaten, bathed and slept with them—never a moment's privacy for 24 hours a day, 7 days a week. We have seen them at their best and at their worst, in good times and in bad. Surely friendships which have survived that supreme test need never be allowed to fade."

Anonymous tank soldier

Prophetic Leader

Your leading article was brilliant in its analysis of what went wrong in Chechnya and what has to be done to put it right. (Comment, September 5th). Save the piece. You will be able to run it exactly as it is, word for word, eight years from now, with just two minor changes—Replace "Russia" with "U.S." and "Chechnya" with "Iraq." However, I am puzzled. If you can be so perceptive in one case, why not in the other? What's the difference?

Trevor Hoyle, Milnrow, Lancashire, England. Letter to the *Sunday Telegraph*, September 12, 2004

A Not to be Forgotten Hero

Admiral Sir Bertram Ramsay was one of the greatest military leaders the Western allies possessed during the Second World War.

He was, more than any other individual, responsible for the miracle of Dunkirk.

He organized Operation Dynamo, which enabled 340,000 allied soldiers to be rescued from behind a shield erected by the gallant (and equally forgotten) First French Army at Lille. With the protection of the British Navy, an armada of small fishing boats set off from the channel ports across the Channel and aided in the evacuation of the remnants of the Regular British Army from France in 1940.

He planned Neptune, the seaborne element of the Normandy landings.

Under his command were more than 6,000 ships, all of which had been allotted tasks amid a timetable of astrophysical complexity. By nightfall on June 6, 1944, 125,000 were ashore. Over the coming weeks his duty was to guard the sea lanes, bearing supplies to the soldiers on the beach head.

It has been proposed to raise a statute in Dover Castle, close to the underground office from which he co-ordinated the miracle of Dunkirk.

Kevin Myers, *Sunday Telegraph*

A War Story

It was a clear, sunny day on the 6th of November, 1940. We were playing soccer at St. John's College playing fields at Paulsgrove, near Portsmouth, in England.

A dog fight started at about 20,000 feet directly overhead. Circling vapour trails crossing and criss-crossing and you could just faintly hear the chattering of machine guns. One plane separated from the rest coming straight down in a perpendicular dive. No flames or smoke. The plane crashed just over the hill from where we were playing. We recognized it as a Hurricane from the shape of the wings.

As soon as the game was finished, we all ran over the hill and found the crash site about 10 yards or so beyond a hedge, in a ploughed farmer's field.

On the other side of the hedge, which was alongside a small country road, there was a soldier from a nearby Ack-Ack (Anti-Aircraft) site standing guard with a rifle.

There was a large smoking crater with some scattered bits of plane wreckage. The soldier came across and spoke to us. We wanted to cross over the hedge and look at the wreckage but this was not permitted. The soldier showed us a piece of foam lining from the pilot's helmet with a hair sticking to it and he told us the pilot's name was Sgt. Pilot John Adair.

In the early 1990's, I read about a retired butcher from the same area who used to place plaques at the site of crashed Battle of Britain pilots and I wrote to him. He responded, indicating that he knew about the above crash—he had seen the plane come down, as he lived nearby at Drayton. He had already placed a plaque near the site. He told me the pilot's official name was H.H. Adair. The butcher's name was Graham Alderson and he invited us to visit next time we were in England.

We visited Graham twice—once in the mid 1990's and again in October, 1998 when he gave me the following information.

The crash site was excavated many years later and the plane's engine was found 14 feet below the surface in solid chalk. Nothing else was found at that time except a bit of helmet. The hole was filled in.

In the 1960's the Tangmere Museum excavated the site and found the engine and one boot, part of a vertebrae, a portion of skull and some rib bones. It was learned that the German pilot who had shot down Sgt. Pilot Adair was named Helmut Wick.*

On our first visit, we saw the site in the ploughed field. When the wheat grows in the field, we were told, you can see the crash site, as the wheat grows differently there.

Graham obtained all of this information through British Air Ministry records and Luftwaffe records. On the 6th of November, 1940, Helmut Wick saw Spitfires above and Hurricanes below and went for the Hurricanes and shot down Sgt. Pilot Adair. Another Hurricane was shot down that day—the pilot was James Tillet and there is a plaque commemorating him at Fareham nearby.

Flying back over the Solent the same day, Wick encountered three Spitfires and shot all three down.

Helmut Wick was himself shot down a couple of weeks later over the sea near the Isle of Wight by a pilot named John Dundas and he himself was immediately shot down by one of Helmut Wick's two wing men—both in Me 109's—behind him.

Over the radio telephone, John Dundas had been heard to say "I've got me a 109." But that was the last thing anyone heard him say.

Another pilot saw one parachute open but no one was ever found—whether it was the German parachute or Dundas is not known.

The British sent out Air-Sea Rescue boats and the German's sent out E-Boats and contacted the RAF via Swiss Red Cross for any news of Wick—but there was no news.

A. Michael Warrington

—See pages of October 5 to 19 in my diary of 1998. The 500 lb. bomb referred to on October 15th came down very close to our home at No. 38 Solent Road, Drayton.

*Wick was the highest scoring ace in the Luftwaffe in the Battle of Britain with 56 victories

---

Another Lifetime—Holland, 1944

This is a story about one of the events described in a book on the history of a road, now called the Riksweg. The history of the road has been described in a book published in Holland called *From Cart Track to Highway*. This road has always been an important connection from Grave to 's-Hertogenvosch (den Bosch). Both these towns have been fortified cities and military camps since the 17th century and especially since the time of Napoleon. This is about some of the events that occurred on the Riksweg in WWII.

In 1944 after Operation Market Garden and the Arnhem conflict, the Riksweg was the western border of the allied corridor to Nijmegen and the British army was tasked with the capture and liberation of den Bosch and the village of Nuland, eight kilometres east of den Bosch, was the first line of German defence.

Extract from the book *From Cart Track to Highway*:

> "The Germans lay ambushes along the Riksweg. Trees
> were blown up and felled across the road and mines
> were placed on both sides of the Riksweg near Nuland.
> Some of the local people were killed stepping on the
> German mines."

After September, 1944, the war actions reached Nuland…the English patrols come and see how the land lies…the Germans counter-attack along the Riksweg…they use people living there as human shields. The local priest, Father Wouter Lutkie, kept a war diary:

"More Germans arrive. Also a group consisting of a police van with a soldier behind it holding a bicycle in one hand and a weapon in the other. He yelled, 'Get into the line! Get into the line!' to everyone he saw. Other soldiers drove the people they came upon the road towards the group behind the van, dragging people out of their houses along the road and destroying doors with the butt end of their rifles. The sick were also dragged out of their houses, as well as little children. The Dutch SS-Man kept yelling 'Get into the line! Get into the line!' In this way some tens of people are being carried along to den Bosch." Between the 4th and 6th of October, 1944 an English reconnaissance unit of the 7th Armoured Division (Desert Rats) scout the German position surrounding Nuland. Second Lieutenant Michael Warrington leads the unit. It exists of two Honey tanks and a scout car. Investigating the area near the crossing Riksweg and the Molenstraet, Lt. Warrington gets shot at by German machine guns. He pulls back towards the crossing. In one of the houses beside the main road the English use a room to make tea, according to good custom and imperturbably between the actions of war.

During one of those breaks a nurse in white uniform suddenly appears, she speaks English well. She refused to provide any information regarding the German positions. She said she was on her way to treat a boy "who got killed by English fire." In spite of being forbidden to go back, she returns to Nuland.

Next day, the nurse, now accompanied by a priest with white hair, comes back to the crossing where the English are positioned. This is Wouter Lutkie. In his war diary he writes about his meeting with Lt. Warrington. He comes with the nurse—Mieke Steins-Bisschop, who was the District Nurse in Nuland at that time—and a man with a wheelbarrow to bury Martinus de Veer, who was killed somewhere along the Riksweg. Nurse Mieke is brought by the English to their command post. Being a priest, Father Lutkie was allowed to continue on his way with his helper.

On 6th of October the Unit scouted the area around the crossing Hoogstraat-Riksweg. Warrington narrates:

General Stuart—'Honey Tank'

"At about half past five in the morning as we reached the group of houses near Heike, we were suddenly hit by an enormous shockwave. Every notion of surroundings, time and place was lost. I thought that I was dead. The next instinctive reaction was to get out of the tank and I jumped off the turret onto the road and into the ditch on the south side of the road opposite the houses. Scoular landed next to me, his eyes wide open with alarm and his headphones still on his head."

After the war, many years later, Michael Warrington returned to Holland to attend a commemoration of the liberation and he met a military historian, Luc van Gent, from den Bosch. Luc had made a film about the liberation of den Bosch. One of the crew members from the Honey, Trooper Dennis Thomas, saw the film in England and contacted Luc who was able to help Warrington and Thomas to get in contact with each other. During a visit to Holland, Warrington started making inquiries and he was put in contact with the local Historical Society. He was able to meet the parents of Martinus de Veer and learned to his great relief that de Veer had not been killed by the English, but by a German shell as he was milking cows in the field.

—Events recorded in *Van Karrenspoor Tot Snelweg (From Cart Track to Highway)*, December, 2005

Vera Lynn

If you can remember "There'll be bluebirds over / The white cliffs of Dover," prepare to raise your glass to the woman who sang it. Dame Vera Lynn will celebrate her 90th birthday in March. I am not the only one of my generation who places her up with those who influenced the outcome of the Second World War.

The dear old BBC of those days began by thinking soldiers fought best on martial music. They were doubtful about a crooner who sang sentimental songs: Too soft.

Vera taught them otherwise. She had two assets. Even over dodgy connections with BBC radio, she could convey to the fighting men that she was singing to him personally, and she could also convey the sense of what Churchill called the "Sunlit Uplands."

There is a line in "Bluebirds" that runs "There'll be love and laughter / And peace ever after." It didn't turn out quite like that, but no matter. On difficult days of that war, it helped to feel it might.

The Imperial War Museum is throwing a birthday party for Vera. It is the right place. She was our secret weapon.

W.F. Deedes, *Weekly Telegraph*, Feb. 27–Mar. 6, 2007

Queen Mother

During World War II, the King and Queen became symbols of the Nation's resistance.

Queen Elizabeth, the Queen Mother, publicly refused to leave London or send the children to Canada, even during the Blitz, when she was advised by the Cabinet to do so. "The children won't go without me, I won't go without the King and the King will never leave."

She often made visits to parts of London that had been targeted by the Luftwaffe, particularly the East End of London, near London's docks. At first there was some criticism because she dressed in expensive clothing. She explained that if the public came to see her they would wear their best clothes. So she should reciprocate in kind. When Buckingham Palace itself was bombed, Queen Elizabeth said, "I'm glad we have been bombed. It makes me feel I can look the East End in the face."

"A Life In Quotes", *The Observer*, March 31, 2002. Also "The War Years", BBC News

I said to the man who stood at the gate of the year, "Give me a light that I may tread safely into the unknown."

And he replied, "Go into the darkness and put your hand into the hand of God. That shall be to you better than light and safer than a known way!"

King George VI (1996–1952)

—In the grim, uncertain early days of World War II the nation listened to King George VI's Christmas message in which he included the above poem

WATER, WATER, EVERYWHERE

To my friends who enjoy a glass of wine…and those who don't.

As Ben Franklin said: In wine there is wisdom, in beer there is freedom, in water there is bacteria.

In a number of carefully controlled trials, scientists have demonstrated that if we drink one litre of water each day, at the end of the year we would have absorbed more than one kilo of Escherichia Coli (E. coli–bacteria found in faeces). In other words, we are consuming one kilo of poo.

However, we do NOT run that risk when drinking wine and beer (or rum, whiskey, gin or other liquor) because alcohol has to go through a purification process of boiling, filtering and/or fermenting.

Remember: Water = poo, Wine = health.

Therefore, it is better to drink wine and talk stupid than to drink water and be full of you know what.

There is no need to thank me for this valuable information: I am doing it as a public service.

Blog written by **Lucian E. Marin** called "Spanish Inquisitor"

WHAT'S IN A NAME?

A young lady was reported as saying, "My name is Patricia and all my life I have been called Patty. I met this fellow and liked him a lot, even enough to marry him, but his surname was POTTIE. No way am I ever going to be Patty Pottie. So I didn't continue the relationship."

Source Unknown

WINSTON CHURCHILL

Referring to Neville Chamberlain

"You were given the choice between war and dishonour. You chose dishonour and you will have war."
"He has a lust for peace."
"In the depths of that dusty soul, there is nothing but abject surrender."

When someone remarked that Mr. Chamberlain, in his effort to make Mr. Attlee (leader of the Labour Party in Britain) accept the Munich Appeasement, resembled a snake dominating a rabbit, Mr. Churchill countered, "It is more like a rabbit dominating a lettuce!"

These words, bitter and true, were spoken just after the Munich settlement of 29th of September, 1938, referring to Prime Minister, Neville Chamberlain.

Neville Chamberlain died in 1940, not long after resigning as Prime Minister and after a long and uncomplaining battle with a serious illness.

Mr. Churchill, now Prime Minister, was profoundly moved and said, "The only guide to a man is his conscience; the only shield to his memory is the rectitude and sincerity of his actions."

The honourable gentleman must try not to develop more steam than he is capable of containing.

I remember, when I was a child, being taken to the celebrated Barnum's Circus, which contained an exhibition of freaks... but the exhibition on the programme which I most desired to see was one described as the "Boneless Wonder." My parents judged that spectacle would be too revolting for my young eyes, and I have waited 50 years to see the "Boneless Wonder" on the Treasury Bench.

—Referring to Ramsay MacDonald, Britain's first Labour Prime
    Minister

General Montgomery to Mr. Churchill during the war. "I neither drink nor smoke and I am one hundred percent fit."

Mr. Churchill: "I both drink and smoke and I am two hundred percent fit."

In defeat; unbeatable;
In victory; unbearable.

Mr. Churchill

—On Field Marshall Montgomery (one of Britain's greatest generals and most successful military leader). Churchill was fond of Montgomery, and Monty remained his faithful friend to the end, visiting him at Chartwell, Churchill's home.

During the North Africa Campaign, the Eighth Army captured the Commander of the Afrika Corps, General von Thoma. General Montgomery, Commanding the Eighth Army, invited the German General to dine with him in his trailer. This upset some people at home in Britain, but Mr. Churchill's reaction was, "I sympathize with General von Thoma—defeated, humiliated, in captivity and…(long pause for dramatic effect) dinner with Montgomery."

<u>Referring to Mr. Attlee</u>

A sheep in sheep's clothing.

He is a modest man who has a good deal to be modest about.

An empty taxi arrived at Number 10 Downing Street and when the door opened, Attlee got out.

Winston Churchill

—These remarks referring to Mr. Clement Attlee were attributed to Mr. Churchill. Mr. Churchill later regretted the last comment particularly and later remarked, "Mr. Attlee is a very nice man."

If Hitler invaded Hell, I would make at least a favourable reference to the Devil in the House of Commons.

—This was an allusion to Hitler invading Russia. Churchill, having often spoken vociferously against the Soviet Regime over the years, was now preparing to help Russia.

―――――――――――

At a reception in Richmond, Virginia, U.S.A. Mr. Churchill's hostess, an ample lady, led Mr. Churchill, the Guest of Honour, to the buffet table. She offered him some cold chicken and he asked her if he could have "breast." As she helped him to a particularly succulent looking piece, his hostess informed him gently that, "We Southern ladies use the term 'white meat.'"

The next day a corsage arrived for her—with the flowers was a card from Churchill on which he had written "I would be most obliged if you would pin this on your 'white meat.'"

Almost 50 years later, Mr. Churchill visited Richmond, Virginia where a sculpture of him was being unveiled. A magnificently Rubenesque lady came up to him and cooed enthusiastically: "Mr. Churchill, I want you to know I got up at dawn and drove a hundred miles for the unveiling of your bust."

Looking upon her generous endowments, Mr. Churchill answered, "Madam, I want you to know that I would happily reciprocate the honour."

―――――――――――

One of Mr. Churchill's famous sparring partners in the House of Commons, and out of it, was Nancy Astor.

On one occasion, when the Astors and the Churchills were guests for a weekend during which Churchill and Nancy Astor argued ferociously the whole time:

Nancy Astor: "If I were your wife I would put poison in your coffee."

Churchill: "Nancy, if I were your husband, I would drink it."

―――――――――――

Newly elected to the House of Commons in 1900, the young Churchill thought a moustache might add dignity and maturity to his youthful looks.

Not long after a woman came up to him and said, "There are two things I don't like about you, Mr. Churchill—your politics and your moustache."

Mr. Churchill replied, "My dear madam, pray do not disturb yourself. You are not likely to come into contact with either."

Mr. Churchill's daughter, Sarah, was first married to a comedian called Vic Oliver. He was considerably older than she, and the Churchills did not really approve the marriage but it went ahead anyway. They became more or less reconciled to it.

At dinner one evening, Vic Oliver wanted to draw out his famous father-in-law. "Who," he asked, "in your opinion is the greatest statesman you ever knew?"

This was a mistake. Mr. Churchill emerged from his gloomy reverie and answered, "Benito Mussolini."

"What? Why?"

"Mussolini is the only statesman who had the courage to have his son-in-law executed."

Mussolini's son-in-law, **Count Ciano**, was his Foreign Minister

----

Leaving the House of Commons bar one evening, Mr. Churchill ran into another woman M.P., the formidable Bessie Braddock.

"Winston," she said icily, "you're drunk."

Mr. Churchill drew himself up, "Madam, you're ugly, but tomorrow I will be sober."

Mr. Churchill was once asked, "If you could not be who you are, who would you like to be?"

Mr. Churchill said, "If I could not be who I am, I would most like to be..." He paused for effect and then, turning to Clementine, his wife, he said, "Mrs. Churchill's second husband."

My most brilliant achievement was to persuade my wife to marry me.

On George Bernard Shaw

An exchange of telegrams:

Shaw: "Two tickets reserved for you, first night Pygmalion. Bring a friend. If you have one."
Churchill: "Cannot make first night. Will come to second night. If you have one."

———————

Unpunctuality is a vile habit, and all my life I have tried to break myself of it.

———————

—Winston Churchill material taken from *The Wicked Wit Of Winston Churchill*, compiled by **Dominique Enright**, and *The Wit & Wisdom of Winston Churchill*, by **James C. Humes**.

———————

WORDS OF WISDOM

Never be afraid to try something new.
Remember, amateurs built the *Ark*, professionals built the *Titanic*.

Source Unknown

———————

Conscience is what hurts when everything else feels good.

Source Unknown

———————

The real art of conversation is not only to say the right thing at the right time, but also to leave unsaid the wrong thing at the tempting but wrong moment.

Dorothy Nevill (1826-1913), English writer

———————

A philosophy professor stood before his class and had some items in front of him. When the class began, without saying anything, he picked up a very large and empty jar and began to fill it with rocks, rocks about two inches in diameter. He then asked the students if the jar was full.

They agreed that it was.

So the professor then picked up a box of pebbles and poured them into the jar. He shook the jar and the pebbles rolled into the open areas between the rocks. He asked the students again if the jar was full. They agreed that it was.

The professor then picked up a box of sand and poured it into the jar. The sand filled up everything else. He then asked once more if the jar was full.

The students responded with a unanimous "Yes."

Then the professor produced two cans of beer from under the table and poured their entire contents into the jar—effectively filling the empty space between the sand. The students laughed.

"Now," said the professor as the laughter subsided, "I want you to recognize that this jar represents your life."

"The rocks are the important things—your family, your partner, your health and your children—things that if everything else was lost and only they remained, your life would still be full."

"The pebbles are the other things that matter, like your job, your house, your car."

"The sand is everything else—the small stuff."

"If you put the sand into the jar first," he said, "there is no room for the pebbles or the rocks. The same goes for your life. If you spend all of your time and energy on the small stuff you will never have room for the things that are important to you. Pay attention to the things that are critical to your happiness. Take your partner out dancing. Play with your children. Take time to get medical check ups. There will always be time to go to work, clean the house, give a dinner party."

"Take care of the rocks first—the things that really matter. Set your priorities. The rest is just sand."

One of the students raised her hand and inquired what the beer represented. The professor smiled and said, "I'm glad you asked. It just goes to show you that no matter how full your life may seem, there is always room for a couple of beers."

Source Unknown

The rainbow after the storm is no guarantee of no more storms. But as there will be storms, so will there be rainbows.

Dr. Stuart Rosenberg

Time is too slow for those who wait,
Too swift for those who fear,
Too long for those who grieve,
Too short for those who rejoice,
But for those who love,
Time is eternity.

Henry van Dyke (1852–1933), American clergyman, educator and author

----

Don't be Afraid to Decline

To sum it all up, there is a time to say yes, and a time to say no. Most of the time, only you can decide. The responsibility is yours, and you must not shirk it.

Source Unknown

Our most precious gems cannot be polished without friction, nor can man be perfected without trials.

(Miss) **E.S. McGillivray**, editor

Wrong is wrong even if everybody is doing it, and right is right, even if nobody is doing it.

Saint Augustine

There are three things which are real: God, human folly and laughter. The first two are beyond comprehension. So we must do what we can with the third.

John F. Kennedy

One thing Ivy taught me—you gotta live like there may not be a "later."

—From the 1998 film *Paulie*, a DreamWorks movie about a funny fast-talking parrot with a big personality (screenplay by **Laurie Craig**).

From a horoscope

However tempted you might be to intervene in a work or family dispute, to do so would be asking for trouble. Refuse to become emotionally involved. Since this is a battle no one can win, stay away from the firing line.

Source Unknown

Only three things give you control of your life—good health, a good education and capital.

Source Unknown

Rose

The first day of school our professor introduced himself and challenged us to get to know someone we did not already know. I stood up to look around when a gentle hand touched my shoulder. I turned around to find a wrinkled little old lady beaming up at me with a smile that lit up her entire being. She said, "Hi, Handsome. My name is Rose. I'm 87 years old. Can I give you a hug?"

I laughed and enthusiastically responded, "Of course you may!" And she gave me a giant squeeze.

"Why are you in college at such a young, innocent age?" I asked.

She replied, "I'm here to meet a rich husband, get married, have a couple of kids…"

"No, seriously," I asked. I was curious what may have motivated her to be taking on this challenge at this age.

"I always dreamed of having a college education and now I'm getting one," she told me.

After class, we walked to the Student Union Building and shared a chocolate milkshake.

We became instant friends. Everyday for the next three months, we would leave class together and talk non-stop. I was always mesmerized listening to this "time machine" as she shared her wisdom and experience with me. Over the course of the year Rose became a campus icon and she easily made friends wherever she went. She loved to dress up and she revelled in the attention bestowed upon her from the other students. She was living it up.

At the end of the semester, we invited Rose to speak at our football banquet. I'll never forget what she said. She was introduced and stepped up to the podium.

As she began to deliver her prepared speech, she dropped her cue cards on the floor. Frustrated and a little embarrassed, she leaned into the microphone and said, "I'm sorry. I'm so jittery. I gave up beer for Lent and this whiskey is killing me! I'll never get my speech back in order so let me just tell you what I know."

As we laughed, she began, "We do not stop playing because we are old. We grow old because we stop playing. There are only four secrets to staying young, being happy and achieving success. You have to laugh and find humour everyday. You've got to have a dream. When you lose your dreams, you die. We have so many people walking around who are dead and don't even know it! There is a huge difference between growing older and growing up. If you are 19 years old and lie in bed for one full year and don't do one productive thing, you will turn 20 years old. If I am 87 years old and stay in bed for a year and never do anything, I will turn 88. Anybody can grow older. That doesn't take any talent or ability. The idea is to grow up by always finding the opportunity in change. Have no regrets. The elderly usually don't have regrets for what we did but rather for things we did not do. The only people who fear death are those with regrets."

She concluded her speech by singing "The Rose."

She challenged each one of us to study the lyrics and live them out in our daily lives.

At the end of the year, Rose finished the college degree she had begun all those years ago. One week after graduation, Rose died peacefully in her sleep. Over 2,000 college students attended her funeral in tribute to the wonderful woman who taught by example that it is never too late to be all you can possibly be.

These words have been passed along in loving memory of Rose. Remember, growing up is optional. We make a living by what we get. We make a life by what we give. God promises a safe landing, not a calm passage. If God brings you to it—He will bring you through it.

Source Unknown

———————————

My grandfather told me the creator gave us two ears, two eyes and one mouth.
He wants you to look and listen twice as much as you talk.

Source Unknown

———————————

The true measure of a person is how he or she treats someone who can do them absolutely no good.

Ann Landers

———————————

Man judges flowers, not by their hues, but by the scent they give;
God judges men, not by their skins, but by the way they live.

Source Unknown

———————————

Never ask a barber if you need a haircut.

Warren Buffett

———————————

Leadership Thought

It is easy to be brave from a distance.

Aesop

No act of kindness, no matter how small, is ever wasted.

Aesop

Be careful the environment you chose, for it will shape you.
Be careful the friends you choose for you will become like them.

W. Clement Stone

Consider the postage stamp: Its usefulness consists of the ability to stick to one thing until it gets there.

Josh Billings

Attitude

We cannot change our past...
We cannot change the fact that people will act in a certain way.
We cannot change the inevitable.
The only thing we can do is play on the one string we have,
And that is our attitude...
I'm convinced that life is ten percent what happens to me.
And ninety percent how I react to it.
And so it is with you...
We are in charge of our Attitudes.

Charles Swindoll

During the 1964 general election in Britain, eggs and flour were flung at Sir Alec Douglas Home. He beamed at his assailants and said not a word. When asked later "Why didn't you respond?" he said, "At my school we were taught that silence is the unbearable repartee."

Source Unknown

Keep your eyes on the stars and your feet on the ground.

Theodore Roosevelt

Forget injuries; never forget kindness.

Confucius

If you refuse to accept anything but the best, you very often get it.

W. Somerset Maugham

Keep your fears to yourself, but share your inspiration with others.

Robert Louis Stevenson

Yesterday is but today's memory, tomorrow is today's dream.

Kahlil Gibran

Idealism increases in direct proportion to one's distance from the problem.

John Galsworthy

The Art of Getting Along

Sooner or later, a man, if he is wise, discovers that life is a mixture of good days and bad, victory and defeat, give and take. He learns that it does not pay to be a sensitive soul, that he should deliberately let some things go over his head.

He learns that he who loses his temper usually loses out. He learns that all men have burnt toast for breakfast now and then and that he shouldn't take the other fellow's grouch too seriously. He learns that carrying a chip on his shoulder is the easiest way to get into a fight. He learns that the quickest way to become unpopular is to carry tales and gossip about others.

He learns that all people are human, and that it doesn't do any harm to smile and say "Good Morning," even if it is raining.

He learns that most of the other fellows are as ambitious as he is and he learns also that they have brains that are as good, if not better, than his; also that hard work and not cleverness is the secret to success. He learns to sympathize with the youngster coming into the business because he remembers how bewildered he was when he first started out.

He learns not to worry when he strikes out because experience has shown him that if he always gives his best, his average will break pretty well. He learns that no man ever got to first base alone, and that it is only through co-operative effort that we move onto better things. He learns that the boss is not a monster trying to work him to death for little or nothing, but that bosses are usually fine men who succeeded themselves through hard work.

He learns that folks are not any harder to get along with in one place than they are in another and that the getting along depends about 98 percent on his own behaviour.

—Baylor University Medical Centre newsletter

A diplomat is a man who always remembers a woman's birthday, but never remembers her age.

Robert Frost

The only man who never makes a mistake is the man who never does anything.

Theodore Roosevelt

Ambition is the path to success.
Persistence is the vehicle you arrive in.

Source Unknown

Life can only be understood backwards.
But it has to be lived forwards.

Kierkegaard

On Growing Up

What's cute in a kitten isn't funny in a cat.

Jackie Cooper, child actor

If all you have is a hammer, everything looks like a nail.

From an original quotation by **Abraham Maslow** (1908–1970)

Lord, you know better than I know myself that I am growing older and will someday be old.

Keep me from becoming talkative and particularly from the habit of thinking that I must say something on every subject and on every occasion.

Release me from the craving to straighten out everybody's affairs. Make me thoughtful but not moody; helpful but not bossy. With my vast store of wisdom it seems a pity not to use it all, but you know, Lord, that I want a few friends at the end.

Prayer that has been attributed to a **17ᵗʰ century nun**

YOUTH

Youth…really cares next to nothing about money, for it has not yet learned what the lack of it means.

Aristotle

THE LAST WORD

The End